PEARSON
COMMON CORE
Literature

Student Companion
All-in-One Workbook

GRADE 7

PEARSON

UPPER SADDLE RIVER, NEW JERSEY • BOSTON, MASSACHUSETTS
CHANDLER, ARIZONA • GLENVIEW, ILLINOIS

Copyright © Pearson Education, Inc., or its affiliates. All Rights Reserved. Printed in the United States of America. This publication is protected by copyright, and permission should be obtained from the publisher prior to any prohibited reproduction, storage in a retrieval system, or transmission in any form or by any means, electronic, mechanical, photocopying, recording, or likewise. The publisher hereby grants permission to reproduce these pages, in part or in whole, for classroom use only, the number not to exceed the number of students in each class. Notice of copyright must appear on all copies. For information regarding permissions, write to Rights Management & Contracts, Pearson Education, Inc., One Lake Street, Upper Saddle River, New Jersey 07458.

Common Core State Standards: © Copyright 2010. National Governors Association Center for Best Practices and Council of Chief State School Officers. All rights reserved.

ISBN-13: 978-0-13-327116-4
ISBN-10:   0-13-327116-1
3 4 5 6 7 8 9 10 V039 17 16 15 14 13

CONTENTS

Comparing Texts: "Stolen Day" by Sherwood Anderson and "The Night the Bed Fell" by James Thurber

UNIT 1 • PART 3 Developing Insights

"Amigo Brothers" by Piri Thomas

"Get More From Competition" by Christopher Funk

"Forget Fun, Embrace Enjoyment" by Adam Naylor

"Video Game Competitiveness" by Jennifer LaRue Huget

"Win Some, Lose Some" by Charles Osgood

© Pearson Education, Inc. All rights reserved.

© Pearson Education, Inc. All rights reserved.

UNIT 3 • PART 1 Setting Expectations

UNIT 3 • PART 2 Guided Exploration

UNIT 4 • PART 3 Developing Insights

The Monsters Are Due on Maple Street by Rod Serling

"All Summer in a Day" by Ray Bradbury

Joseph R. McCarthy *from* Prentice Hall United States History

The Salem Witch Trials of 1692

"Herd Mentality?" by Stephen J. Dubner

© Pearson Education, Inc. All rights reserved.

© Pearson Education, Inc. All rights reserved.

Name _____ Date _____

Unit 1: Short Stories
Big Question Vocabulary—1

The Big Question: Does every conflict have a winner?

attitude: *n.* the opinion or feeling a person has about something

challenge: *n.* something that tests a person's strength, skill, or ability

　　　　v. question or confront; other forms: *challenging, challenged*

communication: *n.* the act of speaking or writing to share ideas; other form: *communicate*

compromise: *v.* agree to accept less than originally wanted; negotiate

　　　　n. an agreement in which people settle for less than they first wanted; other forms: *compromising, compromised*

outcome: *n.* final result of something; conclusion

A. DIRECTIONS: *Write the vocabulary word that best completes each group.*

1. settlement, negotiation, agreement, _____

2. test, trial, competition, _____

3. ending, resolution, answer, _____

4. conversation, correspondence, explanation, _____

5. thoughts, feelings, behavior, _____

B. DIRECTIONS: *Write a dialogue between two friends who are involved in a conflict. Through their discussion, they come to an agreement. Use all five vocabulary words.*

_____

_____

_____

_____

_____

_____

_____

_____

_____

_____

_____

_____

_____

All-in-One Workbook
© Pearson Education, Inc. All rights reserved.

Unit 1: Short Stories
Big Question Vocabulary—2

The Big Question: Does every conflict have a winner?

competition: *n.* a contest between people or teams; other forms: *compete, competing, competed*

danger: *n.* a force or situation that may cause injury; hazard; other form: *dangerous*

desire: *n.* a strong hope or wish for something

      v. to want or hope for something; other forms: *desirable, desired*

resolution: *n.* the final solution to a problem or difficulty; other forms: *resolve*

understanding: *n.* knowledge about something, based on learning or experience

      adj. kind or forgiving; generous; other forms: *understand, understood*

Beth said this to Susan, Becky, and Danielle: "I can't believe that Sharon has decided to enter the race on Saturday. Everyone knows that that's *MY* race, and I'm determined to win it. I thought she was my friend, but I guess I was wrong. I hope someone trips her!"

Each of Beth's friends had a different reaction to what she said.

DIRECTIONS: *Use the word(s) given in parentheses to write what each friend said to Beth.*

(desire, competition)

Susan

(understanding, danger)

Becky

(resolution)

Danielle

© Pearson Education, Inc. All rights reserved.

Name _____ Date _____

Unit 1: Short Stories
Big Question Vocabulary—3

The Big Question: Does every conflict have a winner?

disagreement: *n.* a situation involving a lack of agreement, which may or may not lead to an argument; other forms: *disagree, disagreeing*

misunderstanding: *n.* a mistake caused by not understanding a situation clearly

        v. not understanding something correctly; other form: *misunderstand*

obstacle: *n.* something that makes it difficult for a person to succeed; barrier

opposition: *n.* a strong disagreement regarding an issue; other forms: *oppose, opposed*

struggle: *n.* a long, hard fight against something

        v. to fight hard to succeed in a difficult task; other forms: *struggling, struggled*

A. DIRECTIONS: *Read each passage and follow the directions after it. In your answer, use the vocabulary words in parentheses, or one of their "other forms," shown above.*

1. Ramon tells Jenna to meet him "near the supermarket." Jenna waits for him next to *Brown's Market,* but Ramon doesn't show up. He is waiting near *RightPrice Groceries.*

   Describe this situation. **(misunderstanding, obstacle)** _____

   _____

2. After a long and difficult search, Jenna finally finds Ramon, but she is angry. They argue.

   Describe what takes place. **(struggle, disagreement)** _____

   _____

3. Jenna says that Ramon should have been clearer in his directions regarding where to meet. Ramon doesn't agree.

   Describe what takes place. **(misunderstanding, opposition)** _____

   _____

4. They finally come to an agreement and settle their dispute.

   Use at least two of these vocabulary words to describe the end of the story: **(resolution, understanding, compromise, communication)** _____

   _____

All-in-One Workbook
© Pearson Education, Inc. All rights reserved.
3

Unit 1: Short Stories
Applying the Big Question

Does every conflict have a winner?

DIRECTIONS: *Complete the chart below to apply what you have learned about winners and losers in conflict. One row has been completed for you.*

Example	Type of Conflict	Cause	Effect	Who won or lost	What I learned
From Literature	The competition in "Amigo Brothers"	Two friends both want to win the Golden Gloves championship tournament.	They feel funny around each other at first.	Both boys won because each tried to do his best.	Some conflicts do not have a loser.
From Literature					
From Science					
From Social Studies					
From Real Life					

© Pearson Education, Inc. All rights reserved.

Name _____ Date _____

"Rikki-tikki-tavi" by Rudyard Kipling

Writing About the Big Question

Does every conflict have a winner?

Big Question Vocabulary

attitude	challenge	communication	competition
compromise	conflict	danger	desire
disagreement	misunderstanding	obstacle	opposition
outcome	resolution	struggle	understanding

A. *Use one or more words from the list above to complete each sentence.*

1. People can lose perspective during an intense _____.

2. Their only thought is to eliminate the _____ before them.

3. As a result, they may unintentionally place others in _____.

4. This can make _____ of the battle more complex.

B. *Follow the directions in responding to each of the items below.*

1. List two people whom you know or learned about in school or on the news who were affected by a battle that did not directly involve them.

   _____   _____.

2. Write two sentences describing the battle that affected one of these people, and explain how he or she was affected. Use at least two of the Big Question vocabulary words.

   _____

   _____

C. *Complete the sentence below. Then, write a short paragraph in which you connect this situation to the Big Question.*

Sometimes in a battle, innocent victims _____

_____

_____

_____

_____

_____

_____

_____

© Pearson Education, Inc. All rights reserved.

Name _____ Date _____

"**Rikki-tikki-tavi**" by Rudyard Kipling
Reading: Use Prior Knowledge to Make Predictions

Predicting means making an intelligent guess about what will happen next in a story based on details in the text. You can also **use prior knowledge to make predictions.** For example, if a story introduces a mongoose and a snake and you know that mongooses and snakes are natural enemies, you can predict that the story will involve a conflict between the two animals.

DIRECTIONS: *Fill in the following chart with predictions as you read "Rikki-tikki-tavi." Use clues from the story and your prior knowledge to make predictions. Then, compare your predictions with what actually happens. An example is shown.*

Story Details and Prior Knowledge	What I Predict Will Happen	What Actually Happens
Teddy's mother says, "Perhaps he isn't really dead." I know that Rikki-tikki is the hero of the story, and heroes rarely die during a story.	The mongoose will live.	The mongoose lives.

© Pearson Education, Inc. All rights reserved.

Name _____ Date _____

"Rikki-tikki-tavi" by Rudyard Kipling
Literary Analysis: Plot

Plot is the related sequence of events in a short story and other works of fiction. A plot has the following elements:

- **Exposition:** introduction of the setting (the time and place), the characters, and the basic situation
- **Rising Action:** events that introduce a **conflict,** or struggle, and increase the tension
- **Climax:** the story's high point, at which the eventual outcome becomes clear
- **Falling Action:** events that follow the climax
- **Resolution:** the final outcome and tying up of loose ends, when the reader learns how the conflict is resolved

For example, in a story about a battle, the exposition would introduce the contestants. The rising action might explain the conflict between the contestants and describe events leading up to the battle. The climax might be the winning of the battle by one of the contestants. The falling action could include a celebration of the victory, and the resolution might tell about events that took place in the years following the battle.

DIRECTIONS: *Answer the following questions about the plot elements of "Rikki-tikki-tavi."*

1. Who are the characters, and what is the setting described in the exposition?

_____

_____

2. How do you know that the appearance of Nag is part of the rising action?

_____

_____

3. What happens in the climax of "Rikki-tikki-tavi"?

_____

_____

4. Describe one event in the falling action of the story.

_____

_____

5. What happens in the resolution of "Rikki-tikki-tavi"?

_____

_____

© Pearson Education, Inc. All rights reserved.

"Rikki-tikki-tavi" by Rudyard Kipling
Vocabulary Builder

Word List

cunningly   immensely   mourning   revived   veranda

A. DIRECTIONS: *Use each vocabulary word by following the instructions below. Use the words in the same way they are used in "Rikki-tikki-tavi," and write sentences that show you understand the meaning of the word.*

1. Use the word *revived* in a sentence about a bird.

   _____

2. Use the word *immensely* in a sentence about an activity.

   _____

3. Use the word *veranda* in a sentence about summer.

   _____

4. Use the word *mourning* in a sentence about a dog.

   _____

5. Use the word *cunningly* in a sentence about a board game.

   _____

B. Word Study *The Latin suffix -tion means "the thing that is." Answer each of the following questions using one of these words containing -tion: humiliation, intimidation, justification.*

1. Why would a broken leg be *justification* for sitting out a soccer game?

   _____

2. Why would most people prefer that others not witness their *humiliation*?

   _____

3. If you use *intimidation* to get classmates to vote for you, how are you behaving?

   _____

© Pearson Education, Inc. All rights reserved.

*"**Rikki-tikki-tavi**" by Rudyard Kipling*

Conventions: Common, Proper, and Possessive Nouns

A **common noun** names a person, place, or thing—for example, *president, city, orchestra*. A common noun is not capitalized unless it begins a sentence or is part of a title. A **proper noun** names a specific person, place, or thing; for example, *President Obama, New York City, Los Angeles Philharmonic Orchestra*. Proper nouns are always capitalized.

A **possessive noun** shows ownership. Plural and singular possessives are formed in several different ways:

Type of Noun	Rule	Example
Singular: snake	Add apostrophe -s.	the snake's scales
Singular ending in -s: Carlos	Add apostrophe -s.	Carlos's jacket
Plural that ends in -s: birds	Add apostrophe.	The birds' nest
Plural not ending in -s: people	Add apostrophe -s.	the people's decision

A. PRACTICE: *Underline the nouns in each sentence. Write* C *above each common noun and* P *above each proper noun.*

1. "Rikki-tikki-tavi" is a story in *The Jungle Book* by Rudyard Kipling.

2. He was adopted by a British family living in India.

3. The father says that Rikki-tikki can stay in the house to protect Teddy's family.

4. Rikki-tikki saves the lives of the people by killing Nag and his wife, Nagaina.

B. Writing Application: *Use the noun or nouns in parentheses to answer each question with a complete sentence. When appropriate, form possessive nouns.*

1. Whose cries tell the mongoose that the cobras have killed a baby bird? (Darzee)

   _____

2. Whose gun fires while Rikki-tikki is trying to kill Nag? (Teddy, father)

   _____

3. Rikki-tikki dives into a hole underground. Whose hole is this? (Nag, wife, Nagaina)

   _____

4. Rikki-tikki bites open a large number of eggs. Whose eggs are these, and why does Rikki destroy them? (cobras)

   _____

© Pearson Education, Inc. All rights reserved.

"Rikki-tikki-tavi" by Rudyard Kipling

Writing to Sources: Informative Writing

Use the graphic organizer below to record details from each section of "Rikki-tikki-tavi." Your details should tell *when, how much, how often,* or *to what extent.*

Introduction
Details:

Body
Details:

Conclusion
Details:

Now, use your notes to write a short informative article about mongooses. Write for an audience of third-graders.

© Pearson Education, Inc. All rights reserved.

"Rikki-tikki-tavi" by Rudyard Kipling
Support for Speaking and Listening: Informal Debate

Across the top of this T-chart, write your opinion about mongooses and cobras, stating which animal you find more interesting. Then, record several reasons for your opinion. For each reason, write a fact that supports it. At the bottom of the page, write a sentence summarizing your viewpoint.

My Viewpoint:

Reasons	Facts

Summary: _____

_____

_____

_____

_____

_____

_____

_____

Share your opinion in an **informal debate.**

© Pearson Education, Inc. All rights reserved.

Name _____ Date _____

"Two Kinds" by Amy Tan

Writing About the Big Question

Does every conflict have a winner?

Big Question Vocabulary

attitude	challenge	communication	competition
compromise	conflict	danger	desire
disagreement	misunderstanding	obstacle	opposition
outcome	resolution	struggle	understanding

A. *Use one or more words from the list above to complete each sentence.*

1. It can be a _____ to try to live up to someone else's expectations.

2. People should be free to pursue the goals they truly _____.

3. Through _____, they can reach a(n) _____.

4. That way, their efforts can better achieve a positive _____.

B. *Follow the directions in responding to each of the items below.*

1. Describe a time when you did not live up to someone else's expectations or they did not live up to yours. _____

   _____

2. Write two or three sentences explaining how the preceding experience affected you and the other person involved. Use at least two of the Big Question vocabulary words.

   _____

   _____

   _____

C. *Complete the sentence below. Then, write a short paragraph in which you connect this experience to the Big Question.*

When a person does not live up to someone else's expectations, the loser is _____

_____

_____

_____

_____

_____

© Pearson Education, Inc. All rights reserved.

Name _____ Date _____

Reading: Read Ahead to Verify Predictions and Reread to Look for Details

A **prediction** is an informed guess about what will happen. Use details in the text and your own knowledge and experience to make predictions as you read. Then, **read ahead to verify predictions,** to check whether your predictions are correct.

- As you read, ask yourself whether new details support your predictions. If they do not, revise your predictions based on the new information.
- If the predictions you make turn out to be wrong, **reread to look for details** you might have missed that would have helped you make a more accurate prediction.

> "Of course you can be prodigy, too," my mother told me when I was nine. "You can be best anything."

Details in this passage can help you predict that the narrator's mother will encourage her to become a prodigy. You can read further in "Two Kinds" to check this prediction.

DIRECTIONS: *Complete the following chart. If a prediction in the second column is correct, write* Correct *in the third column. If a prediction is wrong, write* Incorrect *in the third column. Then, in the fourth column, describe what does happen, and include a detail that would have allowed an accurate prediction. The first item has been completed as an example.*

Details in "Two Kinds"	Prediction	Verification of Prediction	Event in Selection and Additional Detail
1. The mother wants her daughter to be "a Chinese Shirley Temple."	The daughter will become the Chinese Shirley Temple.	Incorrect	The narrator fails at being Shirley Temple. "We didn't immediately pick the right kind of prodigy."
2. The daughter begins to think thoughts with "won'ts."	The daughter will rebel against her mother.		
3. The narrator must perform a simple piece "that sounded more difficult than it was."	She will perform well.		
4. The daughter sees her mother's offers of the piano "as a sign of forgiveness."	The daughter will take the piano.		

© Pearson Education, Inc. All rights reserved.

Name _____ Date _____

Literary Analysis: Character and Point of View

- **Character traits** are the individual qualities that make each character unique. These may be qualities such as stubbornness, sense of humor, or intelligence.

- A **character's point of view** is his or her thoughts, feelings, and opinions about what is happening in the story. For example, consider this passage:

  She had come here in 1949 after losing everything in China: her mother and father, her family home, her first husband, and two daughters, twin baby girls. But she never looked back with regret. There were so many ways for things to get better.

This passage illustrates the mother's point of view about her life: She suffered terribly in China, but now that she has come to the U.S., she looks on the bright side. Things can only get better for her, she figures.

A. DIRECTIONS: *After each character's name, write as many adjectives as you can think of that describe that character's traits.*

1. **The daughter:** _____

   _____

   _____

2. **The mother:** _____

   _____

   _____

B. DIRECTIONS: *Finish each pair of sentences about a character's point of view.*

1. From Jing Mei's point of view, her mother wants her to be a genius so that her mother can _____ about her daughter. I can tell this because _____

   _____.

2. From her mother's point of view, Jing Mei could be a genius (at anything) if the girl were willing to _____ _____. I can tell this because

   _____.

3. From her dad's point of view, Jing Mei's performance at the recital is _____. I can tell this because he _____.

4. From her piano teacher's point of view, Jing Mei's performance at the recital is _____. I can tell this because he _____.

© Pearson Education, Inc. All rights reserved.

"Two Kinds" by Amy Tan
Vocabulary Builder

Word List

devastated   expectations   nonchalantly   reproach   sentimental

A. DIRECTIONS: *Think about the meaning of the underlined word in each of these sentences. Then, answer the question in a complete sentence.*

1. Would the daughter have been beyond <u>reproach</u> if she had become a prodigy? Why or why not?

   _____

2. How would the daughter have felt when her mother's expression <u>devastated</u> her?

   _____

3. In what way might a rebellious teenager affect a family's <u>expectations</u>?

   _____

4. What traits identify someone as <u>sentimental</u>?

   _____

5. If a person treats her musical debut <u>nonchalantly,</u> how might she act?

   _____

B. WORD STUDY: *The Latin root -spir- means "breath." Answer each of the following questions, using one of these words containing -spir-: respiration, inspirational, perspire.*

1. If someone's *respiration* is rapid, how is he or she breathing?

   _____

2. What makes a library an *inspirational* place?

   _____

3. When a person is in a gym, what might he or she do in order to *perspire*?

   _____

© Pearson Education, Inc. All rights reserved.

"Two Kinds" from *The Joy Luck Club* by Amy Tan
Conventions: Personal and Possessive Pronouns

A **personal pronoun** takes the place of a noun that names a person.
A **possessive pronoun** is a pronoun that shows possession or ownership.

- If a noun or pronoun is singular, the pronoun that replaces it must be singular.
- If a noun or pronoun is plural, the pronoun must also be plural.
- If a noun or pronoun is feminine, the pronoun that replaces it must also be feminine.
- If a noun or pronoun is masculine, the pronoun must also be masculine.

Personal Pronouns	Possessive Pronouns	Singular and Plural Pronouns	Feminine and Masculine Pronouns
I, me we, us you he, him, she, her, it they, them	my, mine our, ours your, yours his, her, hers, its, their, theirs	Jing-mei plays a <u>song</u>. <u>It</u> doesn't sound very pretty. The book has ten <u>pieces</u> in it. <u>They</u> are easy.	<u>Mr. Chong</u> lives in the building. <u>He</u> is Jing-mei's piano teacher. <u>Jing-mei</u> doesn't try hard. <u>She</u> isn't a genius.

A. PRACTICE: *Underline each possessive pronoun in the sentences below.*

1. Jing-mei doesn't want to practice her piano pieces.

2. Pablo wants to learn about musical composers and their famous works.

3. We received our invitations to the piano recital.

4. Whenever he plays in a recital, Pablo wants his family to come and hear him.

5. When parents push their children too hard, some children may stop trying.

B. WRITING APPLICATION: *Answer each question. Use the pronouns in parentheses.*

1. At the show, how does Jing-mei's performance seem to Mr. Chong? (It, him)
2. What might Waverly think about Jing-mei's piano playing? (She, it)
3. What do the audience members think about Jing-mei's performance? (They, it)
4. Why does Ma give Jing-mei the piano as a gift, in your opinion? (She, it, her)
5. What is the four women's club called? (Their)

© Pearson Education, Inc. All rights reserved.

"Two Kinds" by Amy Tan
Support for Writing to Sources: Journal Entry

For your **journal entry**, put yourself in the place of the character you have chosen. Write that character's name on the line. Jot down specific events in the story. Then, imagine what you see and what you feel, and record those ideas on this chart.

My character:

_____

Event	Details From My Point of View	My Feelings About the Event

Now, use your notes to write a journal entry about the situation.

Name _____ Date _____

Support for Research and Technology: Outline

Use this chart to record information for your **outline** of findings about traditional Chinese beliefs and customs concerning relationships between parents and children.

Father's Role	Mother's Role

Daughter's Role	Son's Role

© Pearson Education, Inc. All rights reserved.

Name _____ Date _____

"The Third Wish" by Joan Aiken

Writing About the Big Question

Does every conflict have a winner?

Big Question Vocabulary

attitude	challenge	communication	competition
compromise	conflict	danger	desire
disagreement	misunderstanding	obstacle	opposition
outcome	resolution	struggle	understanding

A. *Use one or more words from the list above to complete each sentence.*

1. We all would like to have those things that we _____ most.

2. However, a wish come true sometimes creates more _____ than joys.

3. It may even bring you into _____ with others or with your principles.

4. Your _____ toward what you want may change once you have it.

B. *Follow the directions in responding to each of the items below.*

1. List two examples of wishes that could have negative consequences if they came true.

   _____   _____

2. Write two to three sentences explaining how having one of the preceding wishes come true could turn out badly. Use at least two of the Big Question vocabulary words.

   _____

   _____

   _____

C. *Complete the sentence below. Then, write a short paragraph in which you connect this idea to the Big Question.*

   Having wishes come true can sometimes _____

   _____

   _____

   _____

   _____

   _____

© Pearson Education, Inc. All rights reserved.

"**The Third Wish**" by Joan Aiken
Reading: Make Inferences by Recognizing Details

Short story writers do not directly tell you everything there is to know about the characters, setting, and events. Instead, they leave it to you to **make inferences,** or logical guesses, about unstated information.

To form inferences, you must **recognize details** in the story and consider their importance. For example, in "The Third Wish," Mr. Peters finds a swan tangled up in thorns. When he moves closer and tries to free the swan, the swan hisses at him, pecks at him, and flaps its wings in a threatening way. You can use those clues to infer that the swan does not like or trust Mr. Peters.

DIRECTIONS: *The sentences in the left-hand column of this chart offer details about characters in "The Third Wish." (Some of the items are quotations from the story; some are based on the story.) In the right-hand column, describe what the details tell you about the character.*

Detail About a Character	Inference About the Character
1. Presently, the swan, when it was satisfied with its appearance, floated in to the bank once more, and in a moment, instead of the great white bird, there was a little man all in green.	
2. Mr. Peters wishes for a wife "as beautiful as the forest." A woman appears who is "the most beautiful creature he had ever seen, with eyes as blue-green as the canal, hair as dusky as the bushes, and skin as white as the feathers of swans."	
3. But as time went by Mr. Peters began to feel that [Leita] was not happy. She seemed restless, wandered much in the garden, and sometimes when he came back from the fields he would find the house empty. She would return after half an hour with no explanation of where she had been.	
4. After Leita was returned to the form of a swan, she "rested her head lightly against [Mr. Peters's] hand. . . . Next day he saw two swans swimming at the bottom of the garden, and one of them wore the gold chain he had given Leita after their marriage; she came up and rubbed her head against his hand."	

© Pearson Education, Inc. All rights reserved.

"The Third Wish" by Joan Aiken
Literary Analysis: Conflict

Most fictional stories center on a **conflict**—a struggle between opposing forces. There are two kinds of conflict:

- When there is an **external conflict,** a character struggles with an outside force, such as another character or nature.
- When there is an **internal conflict,** a character struggles with himself or herself to overcome opposing feelings, beliefs, needs, or desires. An internal conflict takes place in a character's mind.

The **resolution,** or outcome of the conflict, often comes toward the end of the story, when the problem is settled in some way.

A story can have additional, smaller conflicts that develop the main conflict. For example, in "The Third Wish," a small external conflict occurs between Mr. Peters and the swan that is tangled up in the thorns. As Mr. Peters tries to free the bird, the swan looks at him "with hate in its yellow eyes" and struggles with him. In addition, a minor internal conflict that helps develop the main conflict is Mr. Peters's difficulty in deciding what to do with his three wishes.

DIRECTIONS: *Based on details in each of the following passages from "The Third Wish," identify the conflict as* External *or* Internal. *Then, explain your answer.*

1. [Leita] was weeping, and as he came nearer he saw that tears were rolling, too, from the swan's eyes.

   "Leita, what is it?" he asked, very troubled.

   "This is my sister," she answered. "I can't bear being separated from her."

   Type of conflict: _____

   Explanation: _____

2. "Don't you love me at all, Leita?"

   "Yes, I do, I do love you," she said, and there were tears in her eyes again. "But I miss the old life in the forest."

   Type of conflict: _____

   Explanation: _____

3. She shook her head. "No, I could not be as unkind to you as that. I am partly a swan, but I am also partly a human being now."

   Type of conflict: _____

   Explanation: _____

Name _____ Date _____

"The Third Wish" by Joan Aiken
Vocabulary Builder

Word List

dabbling   presumptuous   rash   remote   verge

A. DIRECTIONS: *On the line, write the letter of the word whose meaning is* opposite *that of the Word List word.*

____ 1. presumptuous
   A. curious   B. modest   C. missing   D. hungry

____ 2. rash
   A. cautious   B. itchy   C. impure   D. hasty

____ 3. remote
   A. casual   B. close   C. faraway   D. controlled

____ 4. dabbling
   A. drooling   B. dipping   C. immersing   D. scratching

____ 5. verge
   A. edge   B. center   C. frame   D. bank

B. DIRECTIONS: *Think about the meaning of the italicized word in each sentence. Then, in your own words, answer the question that follows, and briefly explain your answer.*

1. The old King is *presumptuous* in believing that Mr. Peters will make three foolish wishes. Is the old King overconfident? How do you know?

   _____

2. Mr. Peters is not *rash* in making his wishes. What is he instead?

   _____

3. Mr. Peters lives in a *remote* valley. Is it close to town? How do you know?

   _____

© Pearson Education, Inc. All rights reserved.

"The Third Wish" by Joan Aiken
Conventions: Adjectives and Adverbs

An **adjective** modifies or describes a noun or pronoun. An adjective may answer the questions *what kind? how many? which one?* or *whose?*

In this sentence, *beautiful* modifies *woman*. It tells what kind of woman appeared.

A *beautiful* <u>woman</u> suddenly appeared.

In this sentence, *two* modifies *swans*. It tells how many swans lived near Mr. Peters's home.

Two <u>swans</u> lived near Mr. Peters's home.

An **adverb** modifies or describes a verb. Many adverbs end with *-ly*. An adverb may answer the questions *how?* or *in what way?*

In this sentence, *gracefully* modifies *paddled*. It tells how the swans paddled down the river.

The swans <u>paddled</u> *gracefully* down a nearby river.

A. DIRECTIONS: *Underline the adjective or adjectives in each sentence. Then, circle the noun each adjective modifies.*

1. Mr. Peters drove along a straight, empty stretch of road.

2. He heard strange cries coming from a distant bush.

3. A great white swan suddenly changed into a little man.

4. The grateful stranger granted Mr. Peters several wishes.

5. Mr. Peters soon had a gorgeous wife with pretty blue-green eyes.

B. Writing Application: *Write a sentence in response to each set of instructions.*

1. Write a sentence about Leita, using the adverb *sadly.*

_____

_____

2. Write a sentence about Mr. Peters, using the adverb *lovingly.*

_____

_____

3. Write a sentence about the King of the Forest, using the adverb *gruffly.*

_____

_____

4. Write a sentence about the story ending, using the adverb *peacefully.*

_____

_____

"The Third Wish" by Joan Aiken
Support for Writing to Sources: Anecdote

Use this graphic organizer to help you prepare an anecdote that tells what might have happened if Mr. Peters had not turned Leita back into a swan. In the first rectangle, list details about the new ending that you imagine. In the ovals below it, describe two problems, or conflicts, that might arise as a result of the new ending. Then, in the bottom rectangle, describe one way in which the main character might act to resolve the conflict.

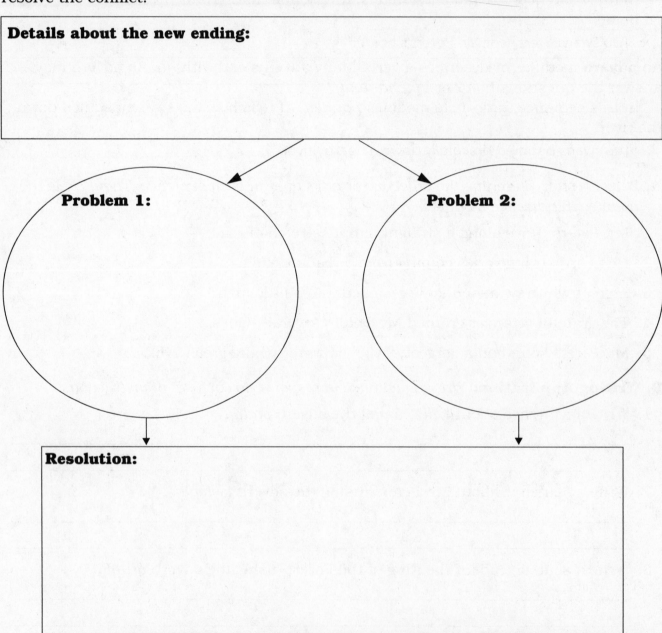

Details about the new ending:

Problem 1:

Problem 2:

Resolution:

Now, use your notes to write an anecdote telling what might have happened as a result the new ending.

© Pearson Education, Inc. All rights reserved.

Name _____ Date _____

"The Third Wish" by Joan Aiken
Support for Speaking and Listening: News Story

What details from "The Third Wish" support the statement that Mr. Peters was good-natured and a doer of good deeds? List three or more details here:

_____

_____

_____

_____

_____

_____

Now, prepare to write a **news story** announcing the death of Mr. Peters and hailing him as a local hero. Choose a method by which to organize your details (for example, strongest to weakest or least important to most important). Name the method here, and organize your details in the three boxes according to that method.

Method of organization: _____

Name _____ Date _____

Writing About the Big Question

Does every conflict have a winner?

Big Question Vocabulary

attitude	challenge	communication	competition
compromise	conflict	danger	desire
disagreement	misunderstanding	obstacle	opposition
outcome	resolution	struggle	understanding

A. *Use one or more words from the list above to complete each sentence.*

1. Different generations can _____ to understand one another.

2. The values of one generation can be in _____ with those of another.

3. It can be a _____ to understand one another's behaviors and beliefs.

4. Even _____ can be difficult because each may view things differently.

B. *Follow the directions in responding to each of the items below.*

1. Describe a time when you or someone you know **struggled** to **communicate** effectively with a member of another generation.

   _____

   _____

2. Explain whether both parties were able to reach an **understanding** and, if so, how. Use at least two of the Big Question vocabulary words.

   _____

   _____

C. *Complete the sentence below. Then, write a short paragraph in which you connect this situation to the Big Question.*

Family members from different generations often do not understand _____

_____

_____

_____

_____

_____

"Ribbons" by Laurence Yep

Reading: Make Inferences by Reading Between the Lines and Asking Questions

An **inference** is an intelligent guess, based on what the text tells you, about things *not* stated directly in the text. One way to make inferences is to **read between the lines by asking questions,** such as, "Why does the writer include these details?" and "Why does the writer leave out certain information?" For example, "Ribbons" opens as Stacy and Ian's grandmother arrives from Hong Kong. The narrator, Stacy, says,

> Because Grandmother's . . . expenses had been so high, there wasn't room in the family budget for Madame Oblomov's ballet school. I'd had to stop my daily lessons.

Why does the writer begin with those details? What conclusion can be drawn? From these details you can infer that Stacy feels some resentment because she has had to give up her ballet lessons so that her grandmother can come from Hong Kong.

DIRECTIONS: *Read the following passages from "Ribbons," and answer the questions.*

1. What inference can you draw from Grandmother's reaction to Stacy's hug?
   When I tried to put my arms around her and kiss her, she stiffened in surprise. "Nice children don't drool on people," she snapped at me.

   _____

2. What can you infer about Grandmother's feelings about her daughter's home?
   Grandmother was sitting in the big recliner in the living room. She stared uneasily out the window as if she were gazing not upon the broad, green lawn of the square but upon a Martian desert.

   _____

3. In the following passage, what inference can you draw from these words, spoken by Stacy's mother, about Grandmother?
   [The girls' feet] were usually bound up in silk ribbons. . . . Because they were a symbol of the old days, Paw-paw undid the ribbons as soon as we were free in Hong Kong—even though they kept back the pain.

   _____

4. In the following passage, what inference about Grandmother can you draw from this attempt to show her affection for Stacy?
   She took my hand and patted it clumsily. I think it was the first time she had showed me any sign of affection.

   _____

5. What inference can you draw from Stacy's description of the invisible ribbon?
   Suddenly I felt as if there were an invisible ribbon binding us tougher than silk and satin, stronger than steel; and it joined her to Mom and Mom to me.

   _____

© Pearson Education, Inc. All rights reserved.

Name _____ Date _____

"Ribbons" by Laurence Yep
Literary Analysis: Theme

A story's **theme** is its central idea, message, or insight into life. Occasionally, the author states the theme directly. More often, however, the theme is implied.

A theme is *not* the same as the subject of a work. For example, if the subject or topic of a story is cultural differences, the theme will be a message about that, such as "cultural differences can be overcome by communication."

As you read, look at what characters say and do, where the story takes place, and which objects seem important in order to determine the theme—what the author wants to teach you about life.

DIRECTIONS: *Answer the following questions about "Ribbons."*

1. What is the setting? Briefly describe it.

   _____

2. What do the main characters say? Summarize the important statements made by Grandmother, Mom, and Stacy.

   Grandmother: _____

   _____

   Mom: _____

   _____

   Stacy: _____

   _____

3. How do the characters act? Describe the important actions of Grandmother and Stacy.

   Grandmother: _____

   _____

   _____

   Stacy: _____

   _____

   _____

4. What objects seem important?

   _____

5. What is the subject, or topic, of "Ribbons"?

   _____

6. Based on your answers above, what would you say is the theme of "Ribbons"?

   _____

© Pearson Education, Inc. All rights reserved.

Name _____ Date _____

"Ribbons" by Laurence Yep
Vocabulary Builder

Word List

coax   exertion   furrowed   meek   sensitive

A. DIRECTIONS: *Complete each sentence with a word from the Word List.*

1. Stacy loved ballet so much that she hardly realized that it was
   _____ until she collapsed from exhaustion after each lesson.
2. Because the binding of her feet was painful physically and emotionally, Grandmother was _____ about her feet.
3. Stacy hoped that she could _____ Grandmother into paying attention to her by explaining her love of ballet.
4. In many cultures it is expected that a daughter will be _____ and
   never challenge her parents' requests.
5. Unsure of what to say to her daughter, Stacy's mother _____ her
   brow in concentration.

B. WORD STUDY: *The suffix* -ious *means "full of." Answer each of the following questions using one of these words containing* -ious: *delicious, harmonious, industrious.*

1. How does an *industrious* worker perform her job?

   _____

2. Why would most people prefer a *harmonious* tune over a dissonant one?

   _____

3. How would a hungry child respond to a *delicious* meal?

   _____

© Pearson Education, Inc. All rights reserved.

"Ribbons" by Laurence Yep
Conventions: Comparison of Adjectives and Adverbs

Using Modifiers (Adjectives and Adverbs) to Show Degrees of Comparison	Examples
Positive Degree: describes something, but does not compare it to anything else	My cat Pokey is a *fast* eater. *(adjective)* Pokey has an *annoying* meow. *(adjective)* Pokey purrs *happily* and sleeps *deeply*. *(adverbs)*
Comparative Degree: compares two things; adds the *-er* ending; uses the word *more* with longer modifiers	My cat Mateo is a *faster* eater than Pokey. *(adjective)* Mateo's meow is <u>more</u> annoying than Pokey's. *(adjective)* Mateo purrs <u>more</u> happily and sleeps <u>more</u> deeply than Pokey does. *(adverbs)*
Superlative Degree: compares three or more things; adds the *-est* ending; uses the word *most* with longer modifiers	My cat Katrina is the *fastest* eater of all. *(adjective)* Katrina's meow is the <u>most</u> annoying of all. *(adjective)* Of my three cats, Katrina purrs <u>most</u> happily and sleeps <u>most</u> deeply. *(adverbs)*

A. PRACTICE: *Underline the adjective or adverb in each sentence. Then, write the degree of comparison it shows:* positive, comparative, *or* superlative.

1. Stacy dances gracefully. _____

2. Ian is younger than Stacy. _____

3. Of the five characters, Grandmother speaks Chinese most fluently. _____

4. Stacy looks more similar to their dad than Ian does. _____

5. Of the five people, Grandmother has had the hardest life. _____

B. WRITING APPLICATION: *Follow the directions for each item. Use the modifier in parentheses. Add the appropriate endings (-er or -est) or words (more or most).*

1. *Write a sentence that compares Stacy's age to Ian's.* (old)

   _____

2. *Write a sentence comparing Grandmother's age to the other characters' ages.* (old)

   _____

3. *Write a sentence comparing the way Grandmother treats Ian to the way she treats Stacy at first.* (lovingly)

   _____

4. *Write a sentence to describe Stacy's dad as he carries Paw-paw's boxes.* (sweaty)

   _____

5. *Write a sentence comparing the way Stacy's mom speaks to Paw-paw to the way Mom speaks to Dad.* (meekly)

   _____

© Pearson Education, Inc. All rights reserved.

"**Ribbons**" by Laurence Yep

Support for Writing to Sources: Response to Literature—Letter to the Author

Remember that you will be writing a **letter to the author**. Tell Laurence Yep whether or not you liked the story, and give specific examples from the story to support your opinion.

First, write a sentence that gives your overall reaction to "Ribbons." Here is one way to think about it: On a scale of ten to zero, with ten being the best and zero the worst, what score would you give this story? Write your overall reaction sentence here:

_____

Next, use the chart below to take notes on your opinions about specific parts of the story. In the third column, you do not have to write in complete sentences. Just get down your ideas:

Quotations From the Story	Page and Paragraph Numbers	My Opinions About Each Part
Example: "Dad tried to change the subject. 'That's Stacy, and this little monster is Ian.'"	page 348, paragraph 9	• Stacy can be boy's/girl's name • Author should tell us right away whether narrator is boy or girl (some boys take ballet) • Don't know for sure that Stacy is girl until Mom says older Chinese people like boys (Ian) better than girls (Stacy)

Use your notes to write your letter. Remember to:

• Organize your letter to reflect correct letter format.
• Establish and maintain a formal writing style throughout your letter.
• End with a brief conclusion that summarizes your ideas and opinions.

© Pearson Education, Inc. All rights reserved.

"Ribbons" by Laurence Yep
Support for Research and Technology: Poster

Answer these questions as you gather information for a **poster** about the benefits of studying ballet.

What is ballet? Define it briefly. _____

_____

_____

_____

_____

What are the basic arm positions? _____

_____

_____

_____

_____

What are the basic foot positions? _____

_____

_____

_____

_____

What are the benefits of studying ballet? _____

_____

_____

_____

_____

"**Stolen Day**" by Sherwood Anderson
"**The Night the Bed Fell**" by James Thurber
Writing About the Big Question

Does every conflict have a winner?

Big Question Vocabulary

attitude	challenge	communication	competition
compromise	conflict	danger	desire
disagreement	misunderstanding	obstacle	opposition
outcome	resolution	struggle	understanding

A. *Use one or more words from the list above to complete the paragraph.*

Competition between people can be healthy, but it can also lead to
_____. If you find yourself one day in _____ with a
friend, be sure to keep the lines of _____ open. If you talk things
through, you can better avoid _____ and can reach a satisfying
_____.

B. *Follow the directions in responding to each of the items below.*

1. List two different times when you experienced a conflict with a friend.

   _____

   _____

2. Write two sentences describing one of the preceding conflicts, and explain what
   helped you resolve it. Use at least two of the Big Question vocabulary words.

   _____

   _____

   _____

   _____

C. *Complete the sentence below. Then, write a short paragraph in which you connect this
situation to the Big Question.*

When a friendship is strong enough, conflicts that arise often _____

_____

_____

_____

_____

_____

_____

"Stolen Day" by Sherwood Anderson
"The Night the Bed Fell" by James Thurber

Literary Analysis: Comparing Characters

A **character** is a person or an animal that takes part in the action of a literary work. In literature, you will find characters with a range of personalities and attitudes. For example, a character might be dependable and intelligent but also stubborn. One character might hold traditional values, while another might rebel against them. The individual qualities that make each character unique are called **character traits.**

Writers use the process of **characterization** to create and develop characters. There are two types of characterization:

- **Direct characterization:** The writer directly states or describes the character's traits.
- **Indirect characterization:** The writer reveals a character's personality through his or her words and actions, and through the thoughts, words, and actions of other characters.

DIRECTIONS: *To analyze the use of characterization in "Stolen Day" and "The Night the Bed Fell," complete the following chart. Answer each question with a brief example from the story. Write* not applicable *if you cannot answer a question about one of the characters.*

Character	Words that describe the character directly	What the character says and does	How other characters talk about or act toward the character
The narrator of "Stolen Day"			
The mother in "Stolen Day"			
Briggs Beall in "The Night the Bed Fell"			
The mother in "The Night the Bed Fell"			

© Pearson Education, Inc. All rights reserved.

"Stolen Day" by Sherwood Anderson
"The Night the Bed Fell" by James Thurber
Vocabulary Builder

Word List

culprit   ominous   perilous   solemn

A. DIRECTIONS: *Read each sentence, paying attention to the italicized word from the Word List. If the word is used correctly, write* Correct *on the line. If it is not used correctly, write a new sentence using the word.*

1. The girl's smile was *ominous* as she happily and gently hugged her new puppy.

   _____

2. The boy was *solemn* after he heard the good news.

   _____

3. The mountain climbers had the most *perilous* stretch at the tip of the peak.

   _____

4. The old lady was considered the most likely *culprit* when her purse was stolen.

   _____

B. DIRECTIONS: *Write the letter of the word that is most similar in meaning to the word from the Word List.*

____ 1. solemn
   A. joyful   **B.** silent   **C.** serious   **D.** cheerful

____ 2. perilous
   A. happy   **B.** tired   **C.** safe   **D.** dangerous

____ 3. culprit
   A. judge   **B.** criminal   **C.** jury   **D.** lawyer

____ 4. ominous
   A. easy   **B.** huge   **C.** threatening   **D.** pleasant

© Pearson Education, Inc. All rights reserved.

"Stolen Day" by Sherwood Anderson
"The Night the Bed Fell" by James Thurber
Support for Writing to Sources: Explanatory Text

Before you **write an essay comparing and contrasting** the narrator in "Stolen Day," and "The Night the Bed Fell," jot down your ideas in this graphic organizer. In the overlapping section of each set of boxes, write details that are true of both characters. In the sections on the left, write details that describe the narrator of "Stolen Day," and in the sections on the right, write details that describe the narrator of "The Night the Bed Fell,"

What are some of each character's traits?

Narrator of "Stolen Day":	Both:	Narrator of "The Night the Bed Fell":

What problems does each character face? How much responsibility does each character have in creating his problem?

Narrator of "Stolen Day":	Both:	Narrator of "The Night the Bed Fell":

What does the character learn from his situation? Which character learns more?

Narrator of "Stolen Day":	Both:	Narrator of "The Night the Bed Fell":

Now, use your notes to write an essay that compares and contrasts the two characters.

© Pearson Education, Inc. All rights reserved.

Writing Process
Autobiographical Narrative

Prewriting: Gathering Details

Now that you have a focused topic, gather details for your narrative by creating a timeline like the example shown.

Event 1: I meet Mark

Event 2: We decide to join the swim team

Event 3: Mark and I compete in the freestyle

Details 1:
Mark has red hair, carries his knapsack everywhere

Details 2:
Cold day—everybody lines up nervously by the pool waiting for the coach

Details 3:
I feel funny about trying to beat Mark. He is probably my best friend.

Event 1:

Event 2:

Event 3:

Details 1:

Details 2:

Details 3:

Drafting: Show, Don't Tell

Bring your story to life by including precise descriptions of places, people, and events and by using dialogue.

1. What specific details can you add to your writing about the person, place, or event?

   _____

   _____

2. How can you make your descriptions of people, places, or events more precise?

   _____

   _____

3. What interesting conversations can you add to your narrative?

   _____

   _____

4. How do these conversations show the characters' feelings and thoughts as they react to events?

   _____

   _____

© Pearson Education, Inc. All rights reserved.

Name _____ Date _____

Writer's Toolbox
Writer's Toolbox: Pronoun-Antecedent Agreement

Pronouns are words that take the place of nouns or other pronouns. The **antecedent** is the word or words to which a pronoun refers. The pronoun you choose must agree with its antecedent in person, number, and gender.

Person	Number	Gender	Pronouns
first person (the person who is speaking or writing)	singular plural	male or female male, female, or both	I, me, my, mine, myself we, us, our, ours, ourselves
second person (the person or people to whom a speaker or writer is talking)	singular plural	male or female male, female, or both	you, your, yours, yourself you, your, yours, yourselves
third person (the person or people about whom the speaker or writer is talking)	singular singular singular singular plural	male female male or female neuter male, female, both, or neuter	he, him, his, himself she, her, hers, herself he or she, him or her, his or hers, himself or herself it, its, itself they, them, their, theirs, themselves

A. DIRECTIONS: *Circle the pronoun in parentheses that correctly completes each sentence. Underline the antecedent with which the pronoun agrees.*

1. Everyone needed to study (his or her, their) notes for the test.
2. Most of the students wrote (his or her, their) notes in spiral notebooks.
3. A few of my friends copied (his or her, their) notes onto computers.
4. Neither Jack nor Leon could find (his, their) notes.

B. DIRECTIONS: *Rewrite these sentences so that they use the correct pronouns.*

1. Most of the students enjoyed his or her art classes.

   _____

2. Carlos was learning the skills that you needed to become a sculptor.

   _____

3. Everyone in the pottery class had their chance to use the potter's wheel.

   _____

4. Either Sonya or Penny had two of their fashion designs made into dresses.

   _____

Name _____ Date _____

Selection Vocabulary

    devastating   evading   perpetual

A. DIRECTIONS: *Decide whether each statement below is true or false. On the line before each item, write TRUE or FALSE. Then explain your answers.*

_____ 1. If a storm is *devastating*, people often work together to rebuild their communities.

_____.

_____ 2. A flower is *perpetual* because it does not last long.

_____.

_____ 3. While *evading* each other's company, the two friends were often found locked in conversation.

_____.

Academic Vocabulary

    communication   conflict   understanding

B. DIRECTIONS: *Complete each sentence with a word, phrase, or clause that contains a context clue for the italicized word.*

1. He showed his *understanding* of the story by _____

_____.

2. We want good *communication* from our political leaders because _____

_____.

3. Antonio and Felix were in *conflict* because _____

_____.

© Pearson Education, Inc. All rights reserved.

Name _____ Date _____

"Amigo Brothers" by Piri Thomas
Take Notes for Discussion

Before the Group Discussion: Read the following passage from the selection.

> The announcer turned to point to the winner and found himself alone.
> Arm in arm, the champions had already left the ring.

During the Discussion: As you discuss each question, take notes on how other students' ideas either differ from or build upon your own.

Discussion Questions	Other Ideas Expressed	Comparison to My Own Ideas
1. Why does the story not name the winner?		
2. What makes both boys "champions"?		
3. Is competition good, bad, or both in this story? Explain.		

"Amigo Brothers" by Piri Thomas
Take Notes for Writing to Sources

Planning Your Informational Text: Before you begin drafting your **analytical essay**, use the chart below to organize your ideas. Follow the directions at the top of each section.

1. Write details about the friends, fighting, and competition.

_____
_____
_____
_____
_____
_____

2. Write the theme that most of the details support.

_____
_____
_____
_____

3. Create categories for the details that support the theme. Write the details in their categories.

_____
_____
_____
_____
_____
_____
_____
_____
_____
_____
_____

© Pearson Education, Inc. All rights reserved.

"Amigo Brothers" by Piri Thomas
Take Notes for Research

As you research **healthy and unhealthy competition,** use the forms below to take notes from your sources. As necessary, continue your notes on the back of this page, on note cards, or in a word-processing document.

Source Information   Check one: ☐ Primary Source   ☐ Secondary Source

Title: _____   Author: _____

Publication Information: _____

Page(s): _____

Main Idea: _____

_____

Quotation or Paraphrase: _____

_____

Source Information   Check one: ☐ Primary Source   ☐ Secondary Source

Title: _____   Author: _____

Publication Information: _____

Page(s): _____

Main Idea: _____

_____

Quotation or Paraphrase: _____

_____

Source Information   Check one: ☐ Primary Source   ☐ Secondary Source

Title: _____   Author: _____

Publication Information: _____

Page(s): _____

Main Idea: _____

_____

Quotation or Paraphrase: _____

_____

© Pearson Education, Inc. All rights reserved.

Name _____ Date _____

"Get More from the Competition" by Christopher Funk
Vocabulary Builder

Selection Vocabulary

deteriorates   maximize   optimal

A. DIRECTIONS: *Complete each sentence with a word, phrase, or clause that contains a context clue for the italicized word.*

1. Erica wanted to *maximize* her time exercising, so she _____

_____.

2. Josh knew he needed to relax before competition to reach his *optimal* performance, so he _____

_____.

3. Because performance *deteriorates* without enough rest, athletes try to _____

_____.

Academic Vocabulary

attitude   outcome   resolution

B. DIRECTIONS: *Follow each direction. Write each response in a full sentence.*

1. Explain why having the right *attitude* is important in competition. _____

_____

2. How does daily practice affect the *outcome* of a competition? _____

_____

3. If competition is like a story, what *resolution* do you want to write for your next competition? _____

_____

© Pearson Education, Inc. All rights reserved.

Name _____ Date _____

Take Notes for Discussion

Before the Partner Discussion: Read the following passage from the selection.

Find your mission and you'll perform at your peak. Just as important, you'll have an enduring sense of satisfaction.

During the Discussion: As your partner discusses each question, take notes on how his or her ideas either differ from or build upon your own.

Discussion Questions	Other Ideas Expressed	Comparison to My Own Ideas
1. Which is more important to Funk, the competition or the **outcome?** Explain.		
2. For Funk, what is more important in competition, the mind or the body?		

© Pearson Education, Inc. All rights reserved.

Name _____ Date _____

Take Notes for Research

As you research **the mind-body connection,** you can use the organizer below to take notes from your sources. As necessary, continue your notes on the back of this page, on note cards, or in a word-processing document.

The Mind-Body Connection	
Main Idea _____ _____ **Quotation or Paraphrase** _____ _____ _____ _____ _____ **Source Information** _____ _____ _____ _____	**Main Idea** _____ _____ **Quotation or Paraphrase** _____ _____ _____ _____ _____ **Source Information** _____ _____ _____ _____
Main Idea _____ _____ **Quotation or Paraphrase** _____ _____ _____ _____ _____ **Source Information** _____ _____ _____ _____	**Main Idea** _____ _____ **Quotation or Paraphrase** _____ _____ _____ _____ _____ **Source Information** _____ _____ _____ _____

© Pearson Education, Inc. All rights reserved.

"Get More from the Competition" by Christopher Funk
Take Notes for Writing to Sources

Planning Your Narrative: Before you begin drafting your **fictional narrative,** use the chart below to organize your ideas. First, identify the character whose point of view you will use. Then follow the directions at the top of each section of the chart.

Character: _____

1. Plan your narrative. Introduce the characters, setting, and the beginning of the plot, according to the point of view of your character.

_____

_____

_____

_____

2. List the plot events from the story. Consider the conflict and how it can be developed. Think about events that would benefit from dialogue, and others that might benefit from vivid descriptive words.

_____

_____

_____

_____

_____

_____

_____

_____

3. Plan the resolution, or conclusion, of the narrative. It should follow from, and reflect back upon, the series of events.

_____

_____

_____

_____

© Pearson Education, Inc. All rights reserved.

"**Forget Fun, Embrace Enjoyment**" by Adam Naylor
Vocabulary Builder

Selection Vocabulary

advocacy   endeavors   trivialness

A. DIRECTIONS: *Revise each sentence so that the underlined vocabulary word is used logically. Be sure not to change the vocabulary word.*

Example: Anyone can <u>explain</u> chess after watching a game for just a few minutes.

Someone must know the game well before trying to <u>explain</u> it to anyone else.

1. The group opposing the new law was pleased by the mayor's <u>advocacy</u> of it.

_____.

2. Jana began paying more attention when she realized the <u>trivialness</u> of the game.

_____.

3. After he fell ill, John increased his <u>endeavors</u> to become a star runner.

_____.

Academic Vocabulary

perceive   explain   opposition

B. DIRECTIONS: *Write the letter of the word or phrase that is the best synonym for the italicized word. Then use the italicized word in a complete sentence.*

_____ 1. *perceive*

    A. disbelieve   C. understand

    B. convince   D. define

_____

_____ 2. *explain*

    A. confuse   C. make longer

    B. clarify   D. make shorter

_____

_____ 3. *opposition*

    A. communication   C. agreement

    B. respect   D. objection

_____

© Pearson Education, Inc. All rights reserved.

Name _____ Date _____

"**Forget Fun, Embrace Enjoyment**" by Adam Naylor
Take Notes for Discussion

Before the Debate: Read the following passage from the selection.

> Words matter. They create cognitive schemas and shape behaviors.
> Fun is the right idea, but the wrong mental message.

During the Debate: As you discuss and debate each question, take notes on how your partner's ideas and those of the opposing team either differ from or build upon your own.

Discussion Questions	Other Ideas Expressed	Comparison to My Own Ideas
1. In contrast to *fun*, what ideas does the word *enjoyment* inspire?		
2. Can words really shape behavior by making a difference in how and why we compete? Cite evidence from the text in your discussion.		

© Pearson Education, Inc. All rights reserved.

Name _____ Date _____

"Forget Fun, Embrace Enjoyment" by Adam Naylor
Take Notes for Research

As you research **how words can affect behavior,** you can use the forms below.
As necessary, continue your notes on the back of this page, on note cards, or in a
word-processing document.

Source Information   Check one: ☐ Primary Source   ☐ Secondary Source

Title: _____   Author: _____

Publication Information: _____

Page(s): _____

Main Idea: _____

_____

Quotation or Paraphrase: _____

_____

Source Information   Check one: ☐ Primary Source   ☐ Secondary Source

Title: _____   Author: _____

Publication Information: _____

Page(s): _____

Main Idea: _____

_____

Quotation or Paraphrase: _____

_____

Source Information   Check one: ☐ Primary Source   ☐ Secondary Source

Title: _____   Author: _____

Publication Information: _____

Page(s): _____

Main Idea: _____

_____

Quotation or Paraphrase: _____

_____

© Pearson Education, Inc. All rights reserved.

Name _____ Date _____

"*Forget Fun, Embrace Enjoyment*" by Adam Naylor
Take Notes for Writing to Sources

Planning Your Argument: Before you begin drafting your **argument,** use the chart below to organize your ideas. Follow the directions at the top of each section.

1. State your claim.

_____
_____
_____
_____

2. Give reasons why you agree or disagree with Adam Naylor.

_____
_____
_____
_____

3. List examples from the text and from your research that support your claim.

_____
_____
_____
_____
_____
_____
_____
_____
_____
_____

4. Jot down notes for your conclusion. Summarize your argument and restate your position.

_____
_____
_____
_____
_____

© Pearson Education, Inc. All rights reserved.

"Video Game Competitiveness" by Jennifer LaRue Huget
Vocabulary Builder and Take Notes for Writing to Sources

Selection and Academic Vocabulary

DIRECTIONS: *Choose the* **synonym,** *or word closest in meaning, to the vocabulary word.*

Selection Vocabulary

_____ 1. *aggressive* A. friendly B. forceful C. anxious

_____ 2. *spur* A. begin B. effect C. cause

_____ 3. *blunt* A. reduce B. demand C. argue

Academic Vocabulary

_____ 4. *deduce* A. conclude B. guess C. know

_____ 5. *insight* A. questioning B. uncertainty C. understanding

Take Notes for Writing to Sources

Planning Your Informational Text: Before you begin drafting your **essay,** use the chart below to organize your ideas. Follow the directions at the top of each section.

1. Plan your introduction. Introduce your main idea. How will you grab readers' interest?   _____   _____
2. List details from the experiments that you will compare and contrast.   _____   _____   _____   _____   _____
3. Write notes on ideas to use in your conclusion.   _____   _____

© Pearson Education, Inc. All rights reserved.

Name _____   Date _____

"Win Some, Lose Some" by Charles Osgood
Vocabulary Builder

Selection Vocabulary

aversion   emerged   impostors

A. DIRECTIONS: *Complete each sentence with a word, phrase, or clause that contains a context clue for the italicized word.*

1. When Marshall said he had an *aversion* to spinach, he meant _____

_____.

2. The women claimed to be photographers for a leading magazine, but we knew they were *impostors* because _____

_____.

3. I could tell she had just *emerged* from the swimming pool because _____

_____.

Academic Vocabulary

attitude   convince   outcomes

B. DIRECTIONS: *Follow each direction. Write complete sentences for your responses.*

1. Name two positive *outcomes* from playing a game of basketball with friends.

_____

_____

2. Describe the best *attitude* to have when preparing to take a test.

_____

_____

3. How might a political leader try to *convince* the public to vote for her in an election?

_____

_____

© Pearson Education, Inc. All rights reserved.

"Win Some, Lose Some" by Charles Osgood

Take Notes for Discussion

Before the Panel Discussion: Read the following passage from the selection.

"For their part, today's sports fans haven't come far from the days of the gladiator . . . whether his team was ahead or behind."

During the Discussion: As the panel discusses each question, take notes on how other students' ideas either differ from or build upon your own.

Discussion Questions	Other Ideas Expressed	Comparison to My Own Ideas
1. What comparisons does Osgood make in the passage?		
2. Who does the author respect more: Tom Landry or Hollywood Henderson? How can you tell?		

© Pearson Education, Inc. All rights reserved.

Name _____ Date _____

"Win Some, Lose Some" by Charles Osgood
Take Notes for Research

As you research **how one of the people faced triumph and loss,** use the forms below to take notes from your sources. As necessary, continue your notes on the back of this page, on note cards, or in a word-processing document.

Source Information   Check one: ☐ Primary Source   ☐ Secondary Source

Title: _____   Author: _____

Publication Information: _____

Page(s): _____

Main Idea: _____

_____

Quotation or Paraphrase: _____

_____

Source Information   Check one: ☐ Primary Source   ☐ Secondary Source

Title: _____   Author: _____

Publication Information: _____

Page(s): _____

Main Idea: _____

_____

Quotation or Paraphrase: _____

_____

Source Information   Check one: ☐ Primary Source   ☐ Secondary Source

Title: _____   Author: _____

Publication Information: _____

Page(s): _____

Main Idea: _____

_____

Quotation or Paraphrase: _____

_____

© Pearson Education, Inc. All rights reserved.

Name _____ Date _____

"Win Some, Lose Some" by Charles Osgood
Take Notes for Writing to Sources

Planning Your Argument: Before you begin drafting your **argument,** use the chart below to organize your ideas. Follow the directions at the top of each section of the chart.

Character: _____

1. State your claim. You will use this in drafting your introduction. _____ _____ _____ _____
2. List opposing claims. Add reasons you disagree with them. _____ _____ _____ _____ _____ _____ _____ _____ _____ _____
3. List facts, reasons, examples, and other evidence from the text that support your claim. _____ _____ _____ _____

All-in-One Workbook
© Pearson Education, Inc. All rights reserved.
55

Orlando Magic by Leroy Neiman
Vocabulary Builder and Take Notes for Writing to Sources

Academic Vocabulary

opposition   conflict   outcome

DIRECTIONS: *Answer each question. Use complete sentences for your responses.*

1. Why might there be *opposition* to closing the community swimming pool early?

   _____.

2. What *conflict* might occur between two friends who are fans of different teams?

   _____.

3. What is one event that might affect the *outcome* of an outdoor tennis match?

   _____.

Take Notes for Writing to Sources

Planning Your Argument: Before you begin drafting your **argument,** use the chart below to organize your ideas. Follow the directions in each section.

1. List ways in which the depiction of competition in the painting is similar to that in the selection.

_____

_____

_____

_____

_____

2. List ways in which the depiction of competition in the painting is different from that in the selection.

_____

_____

_____

_____

_____

© Pearson Education, Inc. All rights reserved.

Orlando Magic by Leroy Neiman
From Text to Topic: Debate

Before the Group Discussion: Study the painting carefully with your team and discuss the debate question: Is this painting mainly about competition, or is it mainly about a specific player?

During the Discussion: As you discuss each question, take notes on how other students' ideas either differ from or build upon your own.

Discussion Questions	Other Ideas Expressed	Comparison to My Own Ideas
1. Who is closer to the ball? Who is closer to the rim? Who is most likely to score? Why?		
2. What techniques does the artist use to show contrast in the painting? What is the significance of the contrast?		

Unit 2: Types of Nonfiction
Big Question Vocabulary—1

The Big Question: What should we learn?

analyze: *v.* to study something's pieces and parts in order to understand it better; other forms: *analyzing, analyzed, analysis*

curiosity: *n.* a desire to learn about or know something; other form: *curious*

facts: *n.* pieces of information that are known to be true; other forms: *fact, factual*

interview: *n.* a meeting in which a person is asked questions

  v. to ask a person questions for a specific purpose; other form: *interviewed*

knowledge: *n.* information and understanding that someone gains through learning or experience; other form: *know*

DIRECTIONS: *List three items as instructed. Then answer each question.*

1. List three questions that arouse your *curiosity.*

   _____   _____   _____

   What might you do to satisfy your curiosity about one of these things? _____

   _____

2. List three famous people whom you would like to *interview.*

   _____   _____   _____

   What would be your first question to one of these people? _____

   _____

3. What *facts* would you use to help a child gain *knowledge* about your state?

   _____   _____   _____

   Which fact would be most interesting to the child? Explain. _____

   _____

4. What three steps might help a student to *analyze* a poem?

   _____   _____   _____

   Why is it important to work carefully when you *analyze* something? _____

   _____

© Pearson Education, Inc. All rights reserved.

Name _____ Date _____

Unit 2: Types of Nonfiction
Big Question Vocabulary—2

The Big Question: What should we learn?

discover: *v.* to uncover information that you did not know before; other forms: *discovery, discovered, discovering*

evaluate: *v.* to decide how good, useful, or successful something is; other forms: *evaluation, evaluating, evaluated*

experiment: *n.* a test that shows why things happen or why something is true

   v. to perform a test to gather new information; other form: *experimenting*

explore: *v.* to discuss or think about something thoroughly; other form: *exploration*

inquire: *v.* to ask someone for information about a topic; other forms: *inquired, inquiring*

A. DIRECTIONS: *Underline the* **synonym** *(the word or phrase closest in meaning) to each vocabulary word.*

1. **discover**	a. test	b. try to see	c. find out
2. **evaluate**	a. judge	b. criticize	c. uncover
3. **experiment**	a. find	b. visualize	c. test
4. **explore**	a. overlook	b. analyze	c. decide
5. **inquire**	a. question	b. consider	c. respond

B. DIRECTIONS: *Complete each sentence by writing the correct vocabulary word in the blank space. Three possible choices are shown in parentheses.*

1. To begin his research on the rings of Saturn, Ramon went to the school librarian to _____ about the facts. *(experiment, inquire, evaluate)*

2. Cheryl performed two tests to _____ the purity of the water. *(experiment, inquire, evaluate)*

3. You can _____ many facts about animals by studying how they interact. *(experiment, discover, explore)*

4. To _____ for clues about its meaning, Jeb and I examined the strange painting carefully. *(explore, evaluate, inquire)*

5. To make his salad more delicious, the chef decided to _____ with different seasonings. *(discover, explore, experiment)*

Unit 2: Types of Nonfiction
Big Question Vocabulary—3

The Big Question: What should we learn?

examine: *v.* to look at something carefully in order to learn more about it; other forms: *examined, examining, examination, exam*

information: *n.* facts and details about a topic; other forms: *informative, inform*

investigate: *v.* to try to find out the truth about something, such as the details of a crime; other forms: *investigation, investigating, investigated*

question: *n.* a sentence or phrase used to ask for information

           v. to have doubts about something; other forms: *questioning, questioned*

understand: *v.* to know how or why something happens or what it is like; other forms: *understood, understanding*

A. DIRECTIONS: *Review the vocabulary words and their definitions. Then write the one that belongs in each group of related words.*

1. knowledge, wisdom, truths, _____

2. check, explore, inquire, _____

3. inspect, study, watch, _____

4. know, learn, grasp, _____

5. challenge, debate, ask, _____

B. DIRECTIONS: *On the line before each sentence, write True if the statement is true, or False if it is false. If the statement is false, rewrite the sentence so that it is true.*

_____1. Most *information* is based on opinions that cannot be proved true.

_____

_____2. If you *examine* the stars through a telescope, you will see them clearly.

_____

_____3. If you don't *understand* the question, you'll probably get the right answer.

_____

_____4. A person who *investigates* a crime is often guilty.

_____

_____5. It is rude and unnecessary to *question* the claims in an advertisement.

_____

© Pearson Education, Inc. All rights reserved.

Name _____ Date _____

Unit 2: Types of Nonfiction
Applying the Big Question

What should we learn?

DIRECTIONS: *Complete the chart below to apply what you have learned about what we should learn. One row has been completed for you.*

Example	Type of knowledge	Why it is important	Effect it will have	What I learned
From Literature	Understanding different cultures, as in "Conversational Ballgames."	To be able to better relate to people who are different from us.	More tolerance and better relationships.	When with people from another culture, don't assume that your own customs are the norm.
From Literature				
From Science				
From Social Studies				
From Real Life				

© Pearson Education, Inc. All rights reserved.

"Life Without Gravity" by Robert Zimmerman
Writing About the Big Question

What should we learn?

Big Question Vocabulary

analyze	curiosity	discover	evaluate	examine
experiment	explore	facts	information	inquire
interview	investigate	knowledge	question	understand

A. *Choose one word from the list above to complete each sentence. There may be more than one right answer.*

1. Anna's _____ about other people helped her learn about different cultures.

2. It can be fun to _____ new neighborhoods in your hometown.

3. Try to ask each new acquaintance at least one _____ about her life.

B. *Follow the directions in responding to each of the items below.*

1. List two different times that you learned something outside of school. Write your response in complete sentences.

_____

_____

2. Choose one of the experiences you listed in number 1. Write two sentences describing that experience. Use at least two of the Big Question vocabulary words. You may use the words in different forms (for example you can change *analyze* to *analyzing*).

_____

_____

C. *Complete the sentence below. Then, write a short paragraph in which you connect this sentence to the big question.*

Our assumptions about unfamiliar experiences are _____

_____

_____

© Pearson Education, Inc. All rights reserved.

"Life Without Gravity" by Robert Zimmerman

Reading: Adjust Your Reading Rate to Recognize Main Ideas and Key Points

The **main idea** is the central point of a passage or text. Most articles and essays have a main idea. Each paragraph or passage in the work also has a main idea, or **key point.**

The main idea of a paragraph is usually stated in a **topic sentence.** The paragraph then supplies **supporting details** that give examples, explanations, or reasons.

When reading nonfiction, **adjust your reading rate to recognize main ideas and key points.**

- **Skim** the article to get a sense of the main idea before you begin reading. Look over the text quickly, looking for text organization, topic sentences, and repeated words.
- **Scan** the text when you need to find answers to questions or to clarify or find supporting details. Run your eyes over the text, looking for a particular word or idea.
- **Read closely** to learn what the main ideas are and to identify the key points and supporting details.

A. DIRECTIONS: *Scan each paragraph below to find answers to the questions that follow.*

Our bodies are adapted to Earth's gravity. Our muscles are strong in order to overcome gravity as we walk and run. Our inner ears use gravity to keep us upright. And because gravity wants to pull all our blood down into our legs, our hearts are designed to pump hard to get blood up to our brains.

1. What parts of the body are discussed in this paragraph?

_____

In microgravity, you have to learn new ways to eat. Don't pour a bowl of cornflakes. Not only will the flakes float all over the place, the milk won't pour. Instead, big balls of milk will form. You can drink these by taking big bites out of them, but you'd better finish them before they slam into a wall, splattering apart and covering everything with little tiny milk globules.

2. What foods are mentioned in this paragraph?

_____

B. DIRECTIONS: *Now, read the paragraphs closely. Answer these questions.*

1. What is the main idea of the first paragraph?

_____

2. What are two details that support that main idea?

_____

3. What is the main idea of the second paragraph?

_____

4. What are two details that support that main idea?

_____

All-in-One Workbook
© Pearson Education, Inc. All rights reserved.
63

Name _____ Date _____

"Life Without Gravity" by Robert Zimmerman
Literary Analysis: Expository Essay

An **expository essay** is a short piece of nonfiction that explains, defines, or interprets ideas, events, or processes. The way in which the information is organized and presented depends on the specific topic of the essay. Writers organize the main points of their essays logically, to aid readers' comprehension. They may organize information in one of these ways or in a combination of ways:

- Comparison and contrast
- Cause and effect
- Chronological order
- Problem and solution

"Life Without Gravity" is an expository essay that explains an idea. It uses cause and effect to make the explanation clear. In the paragraph below, the details help readers understand some of the effects of weightlessness.

> Worse, weightlessness can sometimes be downright unpleasant. Your body gets upset and confused. Your face puffs up, your nose gets stuffy, your back hurts, your stomach gets upset, and you throw up.

DIRECTIONS: *The left-hand column of the following chart names parts of the human body that are affected by weightlessness. In the right-hand column, write the effect—in your own words—as it is described in "Life Without Gravity." If one effect causes yet another effect, describe the second effect as well.*

Body Part	Effects of Weightlessness
The blood	Weightlessness causes _____ _____
The spine	Weightlessness causes _____ _____
The bones	Weightlessness causes _____ _____
The muscles	Weightlessness causes _____ _____
The stomach	Weightlessness causes _____ _____

© Pearson Education, Inc. All rights reserved.

Name _____ Date _____

"Life Without Gravity" by Robert Zimmerman
Vocabulary Builder

Word List

    blander   globules   manned   readapted   spines

A. DIRECTIONS: *On the short line, write* T *if the following statement is true and* F *if it is false. Then, explain your answer in a complete sentence.*

____ 1. Animals' *spines* are very strong.

_____

____ 2. Foods made without pepper are *blander* than the same foods prepared with pepper.

_____

____ 3. All astronauts have successfully *readapted* to life on Earth.

_____

____ 4. *Manned* space flight is considered too dangerous at this time.

_____

____ 5. Floating *globules* help astronauts exercise their muscles in space.

_____

B. WORD STUDY: *The suffix* -ness *from Old English means "the condition or quality of being." Read the following sentences. Use your knowledge of the suffix* -ness *to write a full sentence to answer each question. Include the italicized word in your answer.*

1. What are some of the ways that *weightlessness* is enjoyable?

_____

2. How can living in space cause *feebleness*?

_____

3. Why is it important for astronauts to have a *willingness* to try new things?

_____

© Pearson Education, Inc. All rights reserved.

Name _____   Date _____

"Life Without Gravity" by Robert Zimmerman

Conventions: Action Verbs and Linking Verbs

Verbs are words that express an action (for example, *swim* and *throw*) or a state of being (for example, *am, is, was, felt,* and *seemed*). Verbs that express an action are called **action verbs.**

Jessica *climbed* a mountain.

Verbs that express a state of being are called **linking verbs.** Linking verbs join the subject of a sentence with a word or phrase that describes or renames the subject.

Jessica *seems* strong.

Jessica *is* a mountain climber.

Besides forms of *be* and *seem,* other verbs that can describe or rename a subject are *appear, look,* and *sound.*

A. PRACTICE: *Underline the verb or verbs in each sentence. On the line, identify each verb as an* action verb *or a* linking verb.

1. Astronauts are strong, brave people. _____

2. Weightlessness seems fun, but it causes discomfort. _____,
_____

3. Many astronauts vomit in space, so they dislike weightlessness at first.
_____, _____

4. When milk globs escape, it is maddening. _____,
_____

5. When their tools float away, astronauts feel frustrated. _____,
_____

B. Writing Application: *Write a paragraph telling what you would like most and least about living without gravity. Use at least three action verbs and three linking verbs. Underline each action verb once and each linking verb twice.*

_____

_____

_____

_____

_____

_____

_____

© Pearson Education, Inc. All rights reserved.

Name _____ Date _____

"Life Without Gravity" by Robert Zimmerman
Support for Writing to Sources: Analogy

An **analogy** makes a comparison between two pairs of things that are similar in a certain way, but may be otherwise unalike. A good analogy can spice up your writing, make your readers smile, or explain a difficult concept.

An analogy can take the form of a sentence with two similar phrases joined by the phrase "is like." For example:

Life without gravity <u>is like</u> peanut butter without jelly.

The two phrases before and after "is like" both fit this pattern: **NOUN** without **NOUN.**

Before you write analogies of your own, practice by completing this chart.

A	connector	B
Life without gravity	is like	French fries without ketchup.
Life without gravity	is like	spaghetti without _____.
Life without gravity	is like	(noun) _____ without (noun) _____.
Life without gravity	is like	_____ without _____.
An apple's relationship to an orange	is like	a carrot's relationship to a potato.
An apple's relationship to an orange	is like	a rose's relationship to a _____.
An apple's relationship to an orange	is like	a _____'s relationship to a _____.

On the lines below, write three complete analogies. Use the beginning phrases provided in the chart or come up with your own.

_____

_____

_____

_____

_____

© Pearson Education, Inc. All rights reserved.

Name _____ Date _____

"Life Without Gravity" by Robert Zimmerman
Support for Speaking and Listening: Oral Summary

Use a chart like this one to prepare an **oral summary** of "Life Without Gravity." First, summarize the four most important ideas in the article. Then, for each idea, write down supporting details and a quotation that illustrates the idea. Next, note a visual aid that you might use to illustrate the idea graphically. Finally, write a concluding statement.

Main Idea	Supporting Details	Quotation That Supports Main Idea	Visual Aids That Illustrate Main Idea
1.			
2.			
3.			
4.			

Concluding statement expressing the main message: _____

_____

_____

_____

© Pearson Education, Inc. All rights reserved.

Name _____ Date _____

"I Am a Native of North America" by Chief Dan George
Writing About the Big Question

What should we learn?

Big Question Vocabulary

analyze	curiosity	discover	evaluate	examine
experiment	explore	facts	information	inquire
interview	investigate	knowledge	question	understand

A. *Choose one word from the list above to fill the blanks in the sentences below. There may be more than one right answer.*

1. Many Americans wish to _____ Native American culture.

2. Like many Americans, Chief George has _____ of two cultures.

3. If you could _____ Chief George, what _____ would you ask him?

B. *Follow the directions in responding to each of the items below.*

1. List two different times that you learned something new about your own country. Write your response in complete sentences.

   _____

   _____

2. Choose one of the experiences you listed in number 1. Write two sentences describing that experience. Use at least two of the Big Question vocabulary words. You may use the words in different forms (for example you can change *analyze* to *analyzing*).

   _____

   _____

C. *Complete the sentence below. Use the completed sentence as the beginning of a short paragraph in which you discuss the big question.*

   In order for people to live together in a society, they must _____

   _____

   _____

"I Am a Native of North America" by Chief Dan George

Reading: Make Connections Between Key Points and Supporting Details to Understand the Main Idea

The **main idea** is the most important thought or concept in a work or a passage of text. Sometimes the author directly states the main idea of a work and then provides key points that support it. These key points are supported in turn by details such as examples and descriptions. Other times the main idea is unstated but implied. The author gives you *only* the key points or supporting details that add up to a main idea. To understand the main idea, **make connections between key points and supporting details.** Notice how the writer groups details. Look for sentences that pull details together.

In this passage from "I Am a Native of North America," Chief George states key points and provides details that support the main idea of the essay:

> I am afraid my culture has little to offer yours. But my culture did prize friendship and companionship. It did not look on privacy as a thing to be clung to, for privacy builds up walls and walls promote distrust. My culture lived in big family communities, and from infancy people learned to live with others.

DIRECTIONS: *Write the main idea of Chief George's essay on the line below. Then, read each passage, and write its key point and the details that support it.*

Main idea: _____

And beyond this acceptance of one another there was a deep respect for everything in nature that surrounded them. My father loved the earth and all its creatures. The earth was his second mother. The earth and everything it contained was a gift from See-see-am . . . and the way to thank this great spirit was to use his gifts with respect.

1. **Key point:** _____

2. **Details:** _____

_____

Love is something you and I must have. We must have it because our spirit feeds upon it. We must have it because without it we become weak and faint. Without love our self-esteem weakens. Without it our courage fails. Without love we can no longer look out confidently at the world. Instead we turn inwardly and begin to feed upon our own personalities and little by little we destroy ourselves.

3. **Key point:** _____

4. **Details:** _____

_____

"I Am a Native of North America" by Chief Dan George
Literary Analysis: Reflective Essay

A **reflective essay** is a brief prose work that presents a writer's feelings and thoughts, or reflections, about an experience or idea. The purpose is to communicate these thoughts and feelings so that readers will respond with thoughts and feelings of their own. As you read a reflective essay, think about the ideas the writer is sharing. Think about whether your responses to the experience or idea are similar to or different from the writer's.

In this passage from "I Am a Native of North America," Chief George reflects on life in apartment buildings:

> I see people living in smoke houses hundreds of times bigger than the one I knew. But the people in one apartment do not even know the people in the next and care less about them.

Chief George thinks about how neighbors do not know one another and concludes that they do not care about one another.

A. DIRECTIONS: *In the second column of the chart, summarize Chief George's thoughts about each experience described in the first column. Then, in the third column, write your response. That is, describe your own thoughts on the subject.*

Experience	Author's Thoughts	My Thoughts
1. Chief George describes his grandfather's smoke house.		
2. Chief George's father finds him killing fish "for the fun of it."		
3. Chief George sees his culture disappearing.		

B. DIRECTIONS: *Write the first paragraph of a reflective essay of your own. Include a description of an experience and your thoughts about it. Write on one of these topics:*

- the role of nature in your life
- the importance of tradition in your life
- the meaning of family in your life

_____

_____

_____

_____

_____

© Pearson Education, Inc. All rights reserved.

Name _____ Date _____

Word List

communal   distinct   hoarding   integration   promote

A. DIRECTIONS: *Use the italicized word in each sentence in a sentence of your own.*

1. Chief George seeks to *promote* a greater understanding of Native American culture.

   _____

2. Chief George suggests that *communal* living teaches people to respect one another.

   _____

3. Social scientists can identify many *distinct* cultures in North America.

   _____

4. Native American culture does not prize the *hoarding* of private possessions.

   _____

5. Many peoples see *integration* into American culture as inevitable.

   _____

B. WORD STUDY: *The Latin root -just means "law" or "right." Read the following sentences. Use your knowledge of the Latin root -just- to write a full sentence to answer each question.*

1. If a decision is *unjust*, is it fair?

   _____

2. If there is no *justification* for your mistake, are you free from blame?

   _____

3. Is a *justifiable* complaint one that should be taken seriously?

   _____

"I Am a Native of North America" by Chief Dan George

Conventions: The Principal Parts of Verbs

A verb has four **principal parts**: *present, present participle, past,* and *past participle.* The chart below shows the four principal parts of *learn,* a regular verb. It also shows the principal parts of three irregular verbs. When you use the present participle or the past participle, you include a helping verb such as *am, has, is, are, was,* or *were.* A verb combined with its helping verb is called a *verb phrase.*

	Present	**Present Participle**	**Past**	**Past Participle**
Regular	learn(s)	(am/is/are) learning	learned	(has/have) learned
Irregular	write(s)	(am/is/are) writing	wrote	(has/have) written
Irregular	sing(s)	(am/is/are) singing	sang	(has/have) sung
Irregular	go/goes	(am/is/are) going	went	(has/have) gone

A. PRACTICE: *Underline the verb or verb phrase in each sentence. Then write its principal part.*

1. We are learning about Dan George, a Native North American chief.

   _____

2. Chief George was from British Columbia, Canada.

   _____

3. I am reading his essay about Native North American culture.

   _____

4. In English class, I write essays on many different topics.

   _____

5. We have written six different essays since school started.

   _____

A. WRITING APPLICATION: *Answer each question. Use the principal verb part in parentheses.*

1. What are you learning about in your English class these days? (present participle)

   _____

2. About how many of your relatives have you met? (past participle)

   _____

3. Who was elected president of the U.S. in 2008 and again in 2012? (past)

   _____

4. Where do you go to school? (present)

   _____

5. About how many essays have you written? (past participle) Name one topic you wrote about. (past)

   _____

© Pearson Education, Inc. All rights reserved.

Name _____ Date _____

"I Am a Native of North America" by Chief Dan George
Support for Writing to Sources: Outline

To prepare to write an **outline** of "I Am a Native of North America," create a word web. Write the main idea in the center circle. In each of the circles around it, write a key point. In the circles around each key point, write details that support the key point.

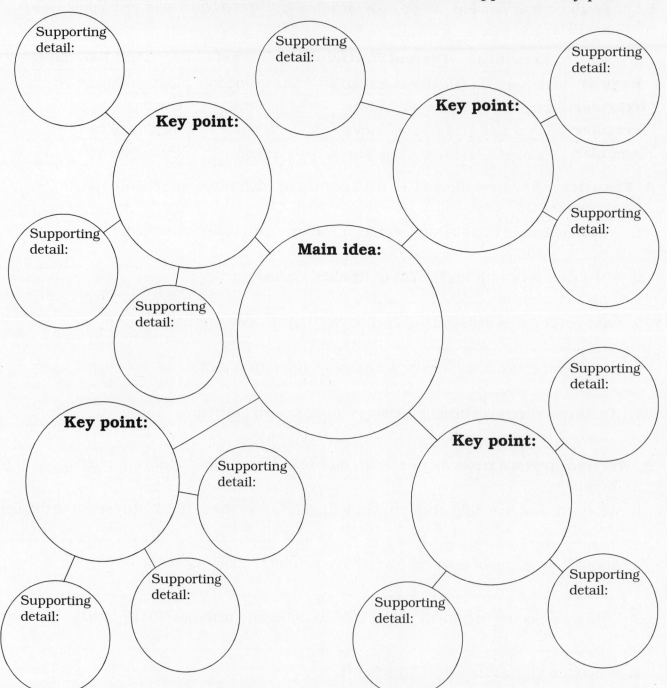

Now, use your word web to make an outline of the essay.

"I Am a Native of North America" by Chief Dan George

Support for Speaking and Listening: Response to Literature

To prepare a **response** to "I Am a Native of North America," write a one-sentence summary of the essay's message. Then, state whether you agree or disagree with the message. Finally, write four reasons that support your response.

Author's message: _____

_____

_____

My response: _____

_____

_____

Reason 1: _____

_____

_____

Reason 2: _____

_____

_____

Reason 3: _____

_____

_____

Reason 4: _____

_____

_____

© Pearson Education, Inc. All rights reserved.

"All Together Now" by Barbara Jordan
Writing About the Big Question

What should we learn?

Big Question Vocabulary

analyze	curiosity	discover	evaluate	examine
experiment	explore	facts	information	inquire
interview	investigate	knowledge	question	understand

A. *Replace the italicized word in the sentence below with one of the vocabulary words above. The meaning of the sentence should stay the same. There may be more than one right answer.*

1. The *details* Barbara Jordan shared in her essay changed the way I saw race relations _____.

2. Barbara Jordan wants us to *study* our own circle of friends _____.

3. It is interesting to *think about* what makes people prejudiced _____.

B. *Follow the directions in responding to each of the items below.*

1. Describe one person you have met who was very different from you. Write your response in complete sentences. Use at least one of the Big Question vocabulary words. You may use the words in different forms (for example you can change *explore* to *exploration*).

   _____

   _____

2. Write two sentences describing what you learned from the person described in question 1. Use at least one of the Big Question vocabulary words. You may use the words in different forms (for example, you can change *analyze* to *analyzing*).

   _____

   _____

C. *Complete the sentence below. Use the completed sentence as the beginning of a short paragraph in which you discuss the Big Question.*

   Asking questions can help _____

   _____

   _____

© Pearson Education, Inc. All rights reserved.

"All Together Now" by Barbara Jordan
Reading: Fact and Opinion

When you read nonfiction, it is important to be able to distinguish between fact and opinion. A **fact** is something that can be proven true. An **opinion** is a person's judgment or belief. It may be supported by factual evidence, but it cannot be proven.

As you read, **recognize clue words that indicate an opinion,** as in the phrases "I believe" and "In my opinion." Also look for words such as *always, never, must, cannot, best, worst,* and *all,* which may indicate a broad statement that reveals a personal judgment. Emotional statements are also often clues to opinion.

You can tell that this statement from "All Together Now" is an opinion because it cannot be proven. Another hint is that it contains the phrase "I don't believe":

> Frankly, I don't believe that the task of bringing us all together can be accomplished by government.

DIRECTIONS: *Identify each of the following quotations from "All Together Now" as a* fact *or an* opinion. *Then, briefly explain your answer. For quotations identified as opinions, point out any words or phrases that indicate it is an opinion.*

1. President Lyndon B. Johnson pushed through the Civil Rights Act of 1964, which remains the fundamental piece of civil rights legislation in this century.

   Fact / Opinion: _____ **Explanation:** _____

   _____

2. One thing is clear to me: We, as human beings, must be willing to accept people who are different from ourselves.

   Fact / Opinion: _____ **Explanation:** _____

   _____

3. Children learn ideas and attitudes from the adults who nurture them.

   Fact / Opinion: _____ **Explanation:** _____

   _____

4. I absolutely believe that children do not adopt prejudices unless they absorb them from their parents or teachers.

   Fact / Opinion: _____ **Explanation:** _____

   _____

5. It is possible for all of us to work on this at home, in our schools, at our jobs.

   Fact / Opinion: _____ **Explanation:** _____

   _____

All-in-One Workbook
© Pearson Education, Inc. All rights reserved.
77

"All Together Now" by Barbara Jordan
Literary Analysis: Persuasive Essay

A **persuasive essay** is a piece of nonfiction that presents a series of arguments to convince readers that they should believe or act in a certain way. Below are some techniques that are often used in persuasive essays. When you read a persuasive essay, be aware of these techniques; you will need to decide whether they are powerful enough to persuade you to accept the author's ideas.

- **Appeals to authority:** using the opinions of experts and well-known people
- **Appeals to emotion:** using words that convey strong feeling
- **Appeals to reason:** using logical arguments backed by statistics and facts

DIRECTIONS: *In the first column of the following chart, copy statements from "All Together Now" that include appeals to authority. In the second column, copy statements that include appeals to emotion. In the third column, copy statements that include appeals to reason. Find at least one example of each kind of appeal.*

Appeals to Authority	Appeals to Emotion	Appeals to Reason

© Pearson Education, Inc. All rights reserved.

Name _____   Date _____

Vocabulary Builder

Word List

culminated   equality   fundamental   optimist   tolerant

A. DIRECTIONS: *Answer each question in a complete sentence. In your answer, use one of the Word List words in place of the italicized word or phrase.*

1. What is the *basic* rule for getting along with others?

   _____

2. What happens when people are not *accepting* of others' differences?

   _____

3. Are you *someone who takes the most hopeful view of matters*?

   _____

4. Barbara Jordan's career *reached its highest point* when she was elected to the United States House of Representatives.

   _____

5. This country was founded on the idea that everyone should enjoy *the same rights*.

   _____

B. WORD STUDY: *The Latin root -leg- means "law." Use your knowledge of the Latin root -leg- to write a full sentence to answer each question. Include the italicized word in your answer.*

1. Is a thief likely to give a *legitimate* account of his actions?

   _____

2. Would you expect an honest person to do something *illegal*?

   _____

3. Is it *legal* to cross the street when the sign reads DON'T WALK?

   _____

© Pearson Education, Inc. All rights reserved.

"All Together Now" by Barbara Jordan

Conventions: Conjunctions and Interjections

A **conjunction** connects two words or groups of words. **Coordinating conjunctions,** such as *and, but, so,* and *or* connect words or groups of words of the same kind. In the examples below on the right, the coordinating conjunctions are **boldface**. The words or groups of words they connect are underlined.

Nouns: Before she ran for office, Barbara Jordan was a <u>professor</u> **and** a <u>lawyer</u>.
Verbs: She <u>campaigned</u> hard **but** <u>lost</u> her first political race.
Groups of words: <u>Jordan lost her race for the Texas House of Representatives</u>, **but** <u>she won a seat in the Texas Senate</u>.

An **interjection,** such as *ouch, wow,* or *oops,* is a part of speech that expresses a feeling such as pain, dismay, or excitement. An interjection may be set off with a comma or an exclamation point. In the examples below on the right, notice how interjections are punctuated and how they can make dialogue sound more realistic.

Pain: Ouch! I bit my tongue!
Excitement: Wow, Ana, that was a really great speech!
Dismay: Oops, I just spilled cereal all over the floor.

A. PRACTICE: *Underline the coordinating conjunction in each sentence. Circle the words or groups of words the conjunction connects. If a conjunction connects single words, identify them as nouns or verbs.*

1. The segregated University of Texas at Austin excluded young Jordan, but Texas Southern University accepted her. _____

2. In debates, Jordan beat competitors from Yale and Brown Universities. _____

3. She excelled in college and graduated with highest honors. _____

4. She graduated from law school and then taught political science. _____

5. Barbara Jordan was a powerful speaker and politician. _____

B. WRITING APPLICATION: *Answer each question. Use at least one of the following interjections with correct punctuation:* wow, whew, well, oh, oh no, hey, boy, yikes, *or* oops.

1. What would you say to your best friend if he or she were elected president of your school?

_____

2. What would you say if you saw a huge wild bear loose in the schoolyard?

_____

3. What would you say if you accidentally stepped on your grandma's cat's tail?

_____

4. What would you say if you ran to class and slid into your seat just as the bell rang?

_____

5. What would you say if you accidentally knocked over something fragile and broke it?

_____

"All Together Now" by Barbara Jordan
Support for Writing to Sources: Persuasive Letter

Prepare to write a brief **persuasive letter** to community leaders, telling them how people in the community can promote tolerance.

Organize your thoughts by completing the chart below. In the left-hand column, write down the goals you would like your government or your community to achieve. In this column, explain any challenges elected officials or community members might face in trying to achieve the goal.

In the right-hand column, describe the persuasive techniques you will use to make each point. Your choices are to:

- **Appeal to authority** by using opinions or experts and well-known people

- **Appeal to reason** by using logical arguments backed by facts

- **Appeal to emotion** by using words that convey strong feelings

Points	Persuasive Techniques

Now, use the ideas you have gathered to write your persuasive letter.

© Pearson Education, Inc. All rights reserved.

"**All Together Now**" by Barbara Jordan

Support for Speaking and Listening: Public-Service Announcement

Use the following prompts as you work with members of your group to prepare a **public-service announcement** encouraging fair treatment of all people.

The message, in brief: _____

_____

_____

_____

_____

Appeal to authority: _____

_____

_____

_____

_____

Appeal to emotion: _____

_____

_____

_____

_____

Appeal to reason: _____

_____

_____

_____

_____

© Pearson Education, Inc. All rights reserved.

"Rattlesnake Hunt" by Marjorie Kinnan Rawlings
Writing About the Big Question

What should we learn?

Big Question Vocabulary

analyze	curiosity	discover	evaluate	examine
experiment	explore	facts	information	inquire
interview	investigate	knowledge	question	understand

A. *Choose one word from the list above to complete each sentence. There may be more than one right answer.*

1. Journalists often _____ dozens of experts before writing an article.

2. Sometimes it's impossible to _____ why some-thing frightens us.

3. The scientist did an _____ to learn how many rattlesnakes he could catch.

B. *Follow the directions in responding to each of the items below.*

1. Write about a time when you learned about something that frightens you. Write your response in complete sentences. Use at least one of the Big Question vocabulary words. You may use the words in different forms (for example you can change *analyze* to *analyzing*).

   _____

   _____

2. Write about a common fear you find difficult to understand. Write your response in complete sentences. Use at least one of the Big Question vocabulary words. You may use the words in different forms (for example you can change *analyze* to *ana-lyzing*).

   _____

   _____

C. *Complete the sentence below. Use the completed sentence as the beginning of a short paragraph in which you discuss the big question.*

   The more we understand something, _____

   _____

   _____

© Pearson Education, Inc. All rights reserved.

Name _____   Date _____

"Rattlesnake Hunt" by Marjorie Kinnan Rawlings
Reading: Evaluate Persuasion: Fact and Opinion

In **persuasive text,** an author tries to persuade, or convince, readers to share his or her opinions. To do a good job of judging such text for yourself, you need to be able to tell the difference between a fact and an opinion. A **fact** is information you can prove. An **opinion** is a judgment.

Fact: Ross Allen is a young herpetologist from Florida.

Opinion: "The scientific and dispassionate detachment of the material and the man made a desirable approach to rattlesnake territory."

Be aware that some writers present opinions or beliefs as facts. To get to the truth, use **resources** such as those described in the chart below to check facts:

Resource	Kinds of Information It Contains
almanac	facts on the climate, planets, stars, people, places, and events updated yearly
atlas	a collection of maps
geographical dictionary	an alphabetical listing of places with statistics and facts about them
dictionary	an alphabetical listing of words with their pronunciations and definitions
encyclopedia	an alphabetically organized collection of articles on a broad range of subjects
reliable Web sites	Internet pages and articles on an extremely wide variety of topics, sponsored by individuals, companies, governments, and organizations

DIRECTIONS: *Read and identify each of these passages as a* fact *or an* opinion. *If the statement is a fact, indicate the best resource for checking it.*

1. Big Prairie, Florida, is south of Arcadia and west of the northern tip of Lake Okeechobee.

   Fact/opinion: _____ **Resource:** _____

2. Snakes take on the temperature of their surroundings. They can't stand too much heat for that reason, and when the weather is cool, as now, they're sluggish.

   Fact/opinion: _____ **Resource:** _____

3. Snakes are not cold and clammy.

   Fact/opinion: _____ **Resource:** _____

4. The next day was magnificent. The air was crystal, the sky was aquamarine.

   Fact/opinion: _____ **Resource:** _____

© Pearson Education, Inc. All rights reserved.

"Rattlesnake Hunt" by Marjorie Kinnan Rawlings
Literary Analysis: Word Choice and Diction

A writer's **word choice** and **diction** are important elements of his or her writing. The specific words a writer uses can make writing difficult or easy to read, formal or informal. Diction includes not only the vocabulary the writer uses but also the way in which the sentences are put together. Here are some questions writers consider when deciding which kinds of words to use:

- What does the audience already know about the topic? If an audience is unfamiliar with a topic, the writer will have to define technical vocabulary or use simpler language.
- What feeling will this work convey? Word choice can make a work serious or funny, academic or personal. The length or style of the sentences can make a work simple or complex.

In this passage from "Rattlesnake Hunt," note that the author uses formal language and difficult vocabulary, but she also uses the informal word *varmints*:

> The scientific and dispassionate detachment of the material and the man made a desirable approach to rattlesnake territory. As I had discovered with the insects and varmints, it is difficult to be afraid of anything about which enough is known.

DIRECTIONS: *Read each passage. Then, on the lines that follow, write down examples of technical vocabulary, formal language, and informal language. If there are no examples of a particular kind of language, write* none.

1. They lived in winter, he said, in gopher holes, coming out in the midday warmth to forage, and would move ahead of the flames and be easily taken.

   Technical vocabulary: _____

   Informal language: _____

   Formal language: _____

2. After the rattlers, water snakes seemed innocuous enough. We worked along the edge of the stream and here Ross did not use his L-shaped steel.

   Technical vocabulary: _____

   Informal language: _____

   Formal language: _____

3. Yet having learned that it was we who were the aggressors; that immobility meant complete safety; that the snakes, for all their lightning flash in striking, were inaccurate in their aim, . . . suddenly I understood that I was drinking in freely the magnificent sweep of the horizon, with no fear of what might be at the moment under my feet.

   Technical vocabulary: _____

   Informal language: _____

   Formal language: _____

© Pearson Education, Inc. All rights reserved.

"Rattlesnake Hunt" by Marjorie Kinnan Rawlings
Vocabulary Builder

Word List

adequate   arid   forage   mortality   translucent

A. DIRECTIONS: *Write* true *if a statement is true and* false *if it is false. Then, explain your answer.*

1. If a region is *arid*, crops will grow there easily.

   True/false: _____ **Explanation:** _____

   _____

2. If a character in a book faces his *mortality,* he believes he will live forever.

   True/false: _____ **Explanation:** _____

   _____

3. If you will be around dangerous animals, it is important to take *adequate* precautions.

   True/false: _____ **Explanation:** _____

   _____

4. *Forage* can be an important part of cattle's diet.

   True/false: _____ **Explanation:** _____

   _____

5. Windows are never *translucent.*

   True/false: _____ **Explanation:** _____

   _____

B. WORD STUDY: *The Latin root -sol- means "alone." Use your knowledge of the Latin root -sol- to write a full sentence to answer each question. Include the italicized word in your answer.*

1. How many people can play a game of *solitaire*?

   _____

2. If you seek *solitude*, do you want others around?

   _____

3. Would many people play a *solo* at one time?

   _____

© Pearson Education, Inc. All rights reserved.

"**Rattlesnake Hunt**" by Marjorie Kinnan Rawlings
Conventions: Subjects and Predicates and Compound Subjects and Predicates

A **simple subject** is a main noun or pronoun. A **complete subject** is a simple subject, plus all the words that modify it. A **simple predicate** is a main verb or verb phrase. A **complete predicate** is a simple predicate, plus all the words that modify it. In the example below, the simple subject is underlined <u>once</u>, the simple predicate is underlined <u>twice</u>, the complete subject is in **boldface** type, and the complete predicate is in *italics*:

The large sleepy <u>rattlesnake</u> *<u>whirred</u> its rattles lightly.*

A **compound subject** contains two or more subjects that share the same verb. A **compound predicate** contains two or more verbs that share the same subject. Both compound subjects and predicates are joined by conjunctions such as *and, or,* and *but.*

<u>Courage *and* experience</u> are essential to the success of a rattlesnake hunt.
"The snake <u>did not coil, *but* lifted its head *and* whirred its rattles lightly</u>."

A. PRACTICE: *For item 1, underline the simple subject once and the simple predicate twice. For item 2, underline the complete subject once and underline the complete predicate twice. For 3, underline compound subjects, and for 4, underline compound predicates.*

1. *Simple Subject/Simple Predicate:* Rawlings wrote an article.
2. *Complete Subject/Complete Predicate:* Her fascinating article tells about a rattlesnake hunt.
3. *Compound Subject:* Rawlings and Allen worked together to catch snakes.
4. *Compound Predicate:* Allen guided Rawlings and taught her hunting skills.

B. WRITING APPLICATION: *Describe a person catching rattlesnakes. Write a first sentence with a compound predicate; use* walked *and* searched. *Write a second sentence with a compound subject; use* rattlesnakes *and* insects. *Write a third sentence with a compound predicate; use* hissed *and* rattled. *Write a fourth sentence with a compound predicate; use* found *and* caught.

_____

_____

_____

_____

_____

_____

_____

_____

Name _____ Date _____

"Rattlesnake Hunt" by Marjorie Kinnan Rawlings
Support for Writing to Sources: Adaptation

Prepare to write an **adaptation** of one of the incidents described in "Rattlesnake Hunt" by completing the following graphic organizer. First note the incident you plan to adapt and the audience you plan to present your adaptation to. For examples, tell the incident to a group of kindergarteners or a class of students learning English. Then, in the first column of the chart, copy down the incident. In the second column, write your adaptation, keeping your audience in mind. Finally, look carefully at your adaptation. See if you can simplify it even further. In the last column, note your revisions.

Incident: _____

Audience: _____

Passage	Adaptation	Revision of Adaptation

You can use your notes to write a final draft of your adaptation.

Name _____ Date _____

"**Rattlesnake Hunt**" by Marjorie Kinnan Rawlings
Support for Research and Technology: Help-Wanted Ad

To prepare to write a **help-wanted ad** for a job as herpetologist (snake scientist) Ross Allen's assistant, fill in this chart.

Job title: _____

Job Responsibilities		Education Required

Experience Required	Skills Required	Traits Required

© Pearson Education, Inc. All rights reserved.

from **Barrio Boy** by Ernesto Galarza
"**A Day's Wait**" by Ernest Hemingway

Writing About the Big Question

What should we learn?

Big Question Vocabulary

analyze	curiosity	discover	evaluate	examine
experiment	explore	facts	information	inquire
interview	investigate	knowledge	question	understand

A. *Choose one word from the list above and use it to complete each sentence. There may be more than one right answer.*

1. Imagine the places you could _____ if you knew how to fly.

2. Actors often like to _____ with different personalities.

3. Anshu seems to _____ her parents' feelings very well.

B. *Follow the directions in responding to each of the items below.*

1. List two different times that you learned something new about your parents. Write your response in complete sentences.

   _____

   _____

2. Choose one of the experiences you listed in number 1. Write two or more sentences describing that experience. Use at least two of the Big Question vocabulary words. You may use the words in different forms (for example you can change *analyze* to *analyzing*).

   _____

   _____

C. *Complete the sentence below. Use the completed sentence as the beginning of a short paragraph in which you discuss the big question.*

Family connections are _____

_____

_____ .

Name _____ Date _____

from **Barrio Boy** by Ernesto Galarza
"A Day's Wait" by Ernest Hemingway
Literary Analysis: Comparing Fiction and Nonfiction

Fiction is prose writing that tells about imaginary characters and events. Novels, novellas, and short stories are types of fiction. **Nonfiction** is prose writing that presents and explains ideas or tells about real people, places, objects, or events. News articles, essays, and historical accounts are types of nonfiction.

In the excerpt from *Barrio Boy,* the writer tells about an actual event in his life. In contrast, the writer of "A Day's Wait" created a narrator who tells about an imagined event in the lives of an imagined father and son.

DIRECTIONS: *Complete the following chart by answering the questions about the excerpt from* Barrio Boy *and* "A Day's Wait."

Question	*from* **Barrio Boy**	**"A Day's Wait"**
1. Who tells the story?		
2. Who are the main characters?		
3. Is there important dialogue? If so, summarize it.		
4. What important events make up the action of the story?		
5. What feelings does the main character have as events unfold?		
6. How is the main character's problem resolved?		

All-in-One Workbook
© Pearson Education, Inc. All rights reserved.
91

from **Barrio Boy** by Ernesto Galarza
"A Day's Wait" by Ernest Hemingway
Vocabulary Builder

Word List

contraption   epidemic   evidently   flushed   formidable   reassuring

A. DIRECTIONS: *Think about the meaning of the italicized word in each question. Then, answer the question.*

1. When there is an *epidemic*, why are infected people kept away from healthy people?

   _____

2. What is an example of a *formidable* school project?

   _____

3. Why might someone call a typewriter a *contraption*?

   _____

4. If Elizabeth is *evidently* healthy, how do you know that she is healthy?

   _____

5. What is a *reassuring* gesture?

   _____

6. When a hunting dog has *flushed* quail from the bushes, what has the dog done?

   _____

B. DIRECTIONS: *For each pair of related words in capital letters, write the letter of the pair of words that best expresses a* similar *relationship.*

____ 1. EPIDEMIC : DOCTORS ::
   A. hospital : nurses
   B. war : soldier
   C. sick : well
   D. medicine : science

____ 2. FORMIDABLE : UNIMPORTANT ::
   A. dangerous : great
   B. square : rectangular
   C. difficult : simple
   D. large : huge

____ 3. EVIDENTLY : SEEMINGLY ::
   A. evidence : trial
   B. slowly : quickly
   C. suddenly : sudden
   D. certainly : surely

© Pearson Education, Inc. All rights reserved.

Name _____ Date _____

from **Barrio Boy** by Ernesto Galarza
"A Day's Wait" by Ernest Hemingway
Support for Writing to Compare Literary Works

To prepare to write an essay that compares and contrasts the narrators of *Barrio Boy* and "A Day's Wait," use this graphic organizer. Respond to each question by jotting down ideas about how the narrators present their stories.

Question	from *Barrio Boy*	"A Day's Wait"
Who is the narrator? What is the point of view?		
What details about the narrator are revealed?		
How is dialogue used in each work?		
How are the narrator's feelings involved in the work?		
What theme do the narrator's thoughts and actions suggest?		
How do other characters affect the narrator?		
How does the narrator bring the story to a close?		

Now, use your notes to write an essay comparing and contrasting the narrators of *Barrio Boy* and "A Day's Wait."

Name _____ Date _____

Writing Process
Argumentative Essay

Prewriting: Gathering Details

Use the following graphic organizer to gather facts, statistics, anecdotes, and quotations from authorities as you conduct research on your topic.

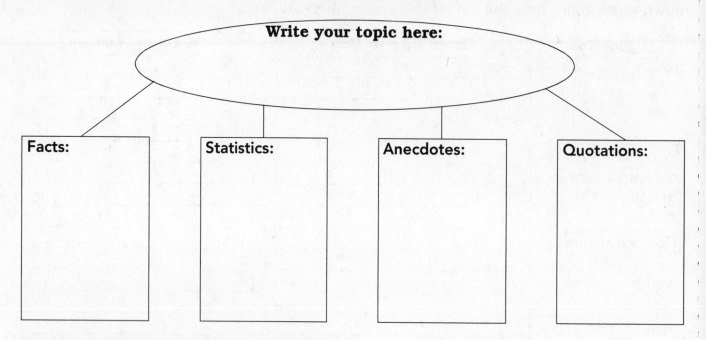

Drafting: Organizing Your Arguments

Use the following graphic organizer to list the supporting evidence you have gathered to support your argument, starting with your least important points at the top and building toward your most important ones.

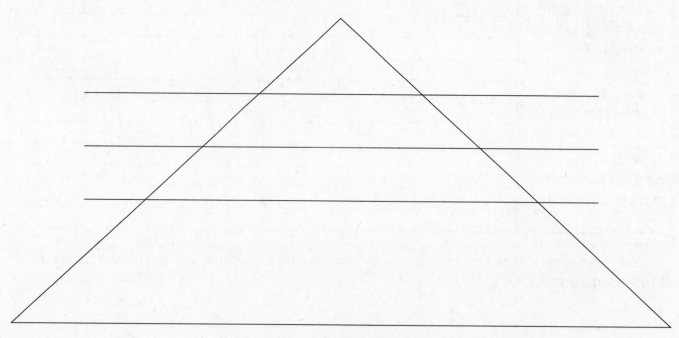

Writer's Toolbox

Conventions: Revising to Combine Sentences Using Conjunctions

A series of short sentences can sound choppy. In addition, the relationships among those sentences may be unclear. You can solve both problems by using conjunctions to combine sentences with related ideas. Study this chart to choose conjunctions that make the relationship clear.

Type of Conjunction	Conjunctions	What They Show
coordinating	and, or, nor	equal relationships
coordinating	but, yet	contrasting relationships
subordinating	although, though, even though, while	contrasting relationships
subordinating	because, since, so that	cause-and-effect relationships
subordinating	after, as soon as, when, until	time relationships
subordinating	where, wherever	spatial relationships
subordinating	if, unless	conditional relationships

Identifying Conjunctions to Combine Choppy Sentences

A. DIRECTIONS: *Circle the conjunction that combines the two clauses into one sentence by best expressing the relationship between the clauses.*

1. Melons taste good, (and, but) most types are very healthy.
2. Bananas are more fattening than other fruits, (or, but) they are also more filling.
3. You can eat apples raw, (or, since) you can bake them.
4. You can lose weight (if, until) you eat low-calorie fruits and vegetables.

Fixing Choppy Sentences

B. DIRECTIONS: *For each item, combine the two choppy sentences into a single sentence that shows the relationship in parentheses. Write your new sentence on the line provided.*

1. (cause-and-effect) Many dieters eat vegetables. They are low in fat.

   _____

2. (contrast) Raw carrots are rich in vitamin A. Cooking them loses some vitamins.

   _____

3. (equal) You can eat spinach raw. You can cook it in a little olive oil.

   _____

4. (time) You must wash and dry raw spinach thoroughly. You add it to a salad.

   _____

© Pearson Education, Inc. All rights reserved.

Name _____   Date _____

"No Gumption" by Russell Baker
Vocabulary Builder

Selection Vocabulary

aptitude   crucial   gumption

A. DIRECTIONS: *Decide whether each statement below is true or false. On the line before each item, write TRUE or FALSE. Then explain your answers.*

_____ 1. I could tell she had *gumption* because she almost never told people what she was really thinking.

_____.

_____ 2. A tornado is approaching, so it's *crucial* to go into the basement until it passes.

_____.

_____ 3. Miguel is an excellent painter; he has a real *aptitude* for it.

_____.

Academic Vocabulary

identify   insight   perspective

B. DIRECTIONS: *Write the letter of the word or phrase that is the best synonym for the italicized word. Then use the italicized word in a complete sentence.*

_____ 1. *identify*

    A. imagine   **C.** recall

    B. recognize   **D.** discover

_____

_____ 2. *insight*

    A. superstitious   **C.** understanding

    B. not able to see clearly   **D.** fearful

_____

_____ 3. *perspective*

    A. knowledge   **C.** belief

    B. an opening or a beginning   **D.** point of view

_____

© Pearson Education, Inc. All rights reserved.

Name _____ Date _____

"No Gumption" by Russell Baker
Take Notes for Discussion

Before the Group Discussion: Read the following passage from the selection.

"Buddy," she said, "maybe you could be a writer."

I clasped the idea to my heart. I had never met a writer, had shown no previous urge to write, and hadn't a notion how to become a writer, but I loved stories and thought that making up stories must surely be almost as much fun as reading them. Best of all, though, and what really gladdened my heart, was the ease of the writer's life. Writers did not have to trudge through the town peddling from canvas bags, defending themselves against angry dogs, being rejected by surly strangers. Writers did not have to ring doorbells. So far as I could make out, what writers did couldn't even be classified as work.

During the Discussion: As you discuss each question, take notes on how other students' ideas either differ from or build upon your own.

Discussion Questions	Other Ideas Expressed	Comparison to My Own Ideas
1. How does this passage show Baker's sense of humor?		
2. How does Baker's sense of humor impact his writing career?		

"No Gumption" by Russell Baker
Take Notes for Writing to Sources

Planning Your Argument: Before you begin drafting your **persuasive essay,** use the chart below to organize your ideas. Follow the directions at the top of each section.

1. State your claim. You will use this to draft your introduction.

_____

_____

_____

2. List opposing arguments. You will want to acknowledge them and give reasons why you disagree in the body of your essay.

_____

_____

_____

3. List details and evidence from the text that support your claim.

_____

_____

_____

_____

_____

_____

_____

_____

4. Jot down notes for your conclusion. Summarize your argument and restate your position.

_____

_____

_____

Name _____ Date _____

As you research **the relationship between goals and motivation,** use the forms below to take notes from your sources. As necessary, continue your notes on the back of this page, on note cards, or in a word-processing document.

Source Information   Check one: ☐ Primary Source   ☐ Secondary Source

Title: _____   Author: _____

Publication Information: _____

Page(s): _____

Main Idea: _____

_____

Quotation or Paraphrase: _____

_____

Source Information   Check one: ☐ Primary Source   ☐ Secondary Source

Title: _____   Author: _____

Publication Information: _____

Page(s): _____

Main Idea: _____

_____

Quotation or Paraphrase: _____

_____

Source Information   Check one: ☐ Primary Source   ☐ Secondary Source

Title: _____   Author: _____

Publication Information: _____

Page(s): _____

Main Idea: _____

_____

Quotation or Paraphrase: _____

_____

© Pearson Education, Inc. All rights reserved.

"Intrinsic Motivation Doesn't Exist" by Jeff Grabmeier
Vocabulary Builder

Selection Vocabulary

extrinsic   intrinsic   psychologists

A. DIRECTIONS: *Follow each direction. Write each response in a full sentence.*

1. Suggest a reason that people visit *psychologists.* _____

_____.

2. Give an example of an *intrinsic* motivation and explain why it is *intrinsic.* _____

_____.

3. Give an example of an *extrinsic* motivation and explain why it is *extrinsic.* _____

_____.

Academic Vocabulary

bias   investigate   perceptions

B. DIRECTIONS: *Write at least one synonym, one antonym, and an example sentence for each word. Synonyms and antonyms can be words or phrases.*

Word	Synonym	Antonym	Example Sentence
perception			
bias			
investigate			

© Pearson Education, Inc. All rights reserved.

Name _____ Date _____

"Intrinsic Motivation Doesn't Exist" by Jeff Grabmeier
Take Notes for Discussion

Before the Group Discussion: Read the following passage from the selection.

"There is no reason that money can't be an effective motivator, or that grades can't motivate students in school," he said. "It's all a matter of individual differences. Different people are motivated in different ways."

During the Discussion: As you discuss and debate each question, take notes on how other students' ideas either differ from or build upon your own.

Discussion Questions	Other Ideas Expressed	Comparison to My Own Ideas
1. How does Reiss feel about money as a motivator?		
2. What does Reiss believe about how people are motivated?		

© Pearson Education, Inc. All rights reserved.

Name _____ Date _____

"Intrinsic Motivation Doesn't Exist" by Jeff Grabmeier
Take Notes for Research

As you research **what experts say about paying students for getting good grades,** use the chart below to take notes from your sources. As necessary, continue your notes on the back of this page, on note cards, or in a word-processing document.

Experts on the Benefits of Paying Students to Get Good Grades

Main Idea _____

_____

Quotation or Paraphrase _____

_____

_____

_____

Source Information _____

_____

_____

_____

Main Idea _____

_____

Quotation or Paraphrase _____

_____

_____

_____

Source Information _____

_____

_____

_____

Main Idea _____

_____

Quotation or Paraphrase _____

_____

_____

_____

Source Information _____

_____

_____

_____

Main Idea _____

_____

Quotation or Paraphrase _____

_____

_____

_____

Source Information _____

_____

_____

_____

© Pearson Education, Inc. All rights reserved.

"Intrinsic Motivation Doesn't Exist" by Jeff Grabmeier

Take Notes for Writing to Sources

Planning Your Argument: Before you begin drafting your **argument,** use the chart below to organize your ideas. Follow the directions in each section.

---

1. State your position on whether or not extrinsic rewards are good motivators. You will use this to draft your thesis statement.

_____

_____

_____

---

2. List points of evidence to support your position: strong reasoning and textual facts and details.

_____

_____

_____

_____

_____

_____

_____

_____

_____

---

3. List reasons someone might have for an opposing view. You will need to refute these reasons in your essay.

_____

_____

_____

_____

_____

---

4. Jot down notes for your conclusion. Summarize your argument and restate your position.

_____

_____

_____

© Pearson Education, Inc. All rights reserved.

"The Cremation of Sam McGee" by Robert Service
Vocabulary Builder

Selection Vocabulary

cremated   loathed   whimper

A. DIRECTIONS: *Complete each sentence with a word, phrase, or clause that contains a context clue for the italicized word.*

1. Sam McGee was *cremated* on the shore of Lake LaBarge because _____

   _____.

2. A dog might *whimper* if it _____

   _____?

3. The narrator *loathed* seeing Sam McGee burn because _____

   _____

Academic Vocabulary

contribute   images   outcome

B. DIRECTIONS: *Follow each direction. Write complete sentences for your responses.*

1. What is the most vivid mental *image* you remember from the poem, "The Cremation of Sam McGee"?

   _____

   _____

2. How might a dog *contribute* to the wellbeing of someone?

   _____

   _____

3. What would be a good *outcome* for someone caught outside in the bitter cold?

   _____

   _____

"The Cremation of Sam McGee" by Robert Service
Take Notes for Discussion

Before the Partner Discussion: Read the following passage from the selection.

> I do not know how long in the snow
>   I wrestled with grisly fear;
> But the stars came out and they danced about
>   ere again I ventured near;
> I was sick with dread, but I bravely said:
>   "I'll just take a peep inside.
> I guess he's cooked, and it's time I looked"; . . .
>   then the door I opened wide.

During the Discussion: As you and your partner discuss each question, take notes on how your partner's ideas either differ from or build upon your own.

Discussion Questions	Other Ideas Expressed	Comparison to My Own Ideas
1. Why is the speaker afraid in this passage?		
2. How do the words *cooked* and *looked* create humor here?		

© Pearson Education, Inc. All rights reserved.

Name _____ Date _____

"The Cremation of Sam McGee" by Robert Service
Take Notes for Research

As you research **the Klondike Gold Rush,** use the forms below to take notes from your sources. As necessary, continue your notes on the back of this page, on note cards, or in a word-processing document.

Source Information   Check one: ☐ Primary Source   ☐ Secondary Source

Title: _____   Author: _____

Publication Information: _____

Page(s): _____

Main Idea: _____

_____

Quotation or Paraphrase: _____

_____

Source Information   Check one: ☐ Primary Source   ☐ Secondary Source

Title: _____   Author: _____

Publication Information: _____

Page(s): _____

Main Idea: _____

_____

Quotation or Paraphrase: _____

_____

Source Information   Check one: ☐ Primary Source   ☐ Secondary Source

Title: _____   Author: _____

Publication Information: _____

Page(s): _____

Main Idea: _____

_____

Quotation or Paraphrase: _____

_____

© Pearson Education, Inc. All rights reserved.

Name _____   Date _____

Take Notes for Writing to Sources

Planning Your Narrative: Before you begin drafting your **fictional narrative,** use the chart below to organize your ideas. First, identify the character whose point of view you will use. Then follow the directions at the top of each section of the chart.

Character: _____

---

1. Plan your narrative. Establish your main character and introduce the other characters, the setting, and the beginning of the plot, according to the point of view of your character.

_____

_____

_____

_____

---

2. List the plot events for your story. Think about how certain events might benefit from vivid descriptive words.

_____

_____

_____

_____

_____

_____

_____

_____

_____

_____

---

3. Plan the conclusion of the narrative. It should follow from, and reflect back upon, the series of events.

_____

_____

_____

_____

© Pearson Education, Inc. All rights reserved.

Name _____ Date _____

"A Special Gift–The Legacy of 'Snowflake' Bentley" by Barbara Eaglesham
Vocabulary Builder

Selection Vocabulary

      evaporated   hexagons   negatives

A. DIRECTIONS: *Use the italicized word in each sentence in a sentence of your own.*

1. Every math student has studied *hexagons.* _____

    _____.

2. The snow crystals *evaporated.* _____

    _____.

3. *Negatives* must not get wet. _____

    _____.

Academic Vocabulary

      focus   inquiry   observe

B. DIRECTIONS: *Complete each sentence with a word, phrase, or clause that contains a context clue for the italicized word.*

1. If you regularly *observe* the sky _____

    _____.

2. Samantha adjusted the *focus* of the telescope because _____

    _____.

3. Eric emailed an *inquiry* to a scientist because _____

    _____.

© Pearson Education, Inc. All rights reserved.

Name _____ Date _____

"A Special Gift–The Legacy of 'Snowflake' Bentley" by Barbara Eaglesham
Take Notes for Discussion

Before the Partner Discussion: Read the following passage from the selection.

> Bentley's book, *Snow Crystals,* containing 2,453 of his photographs, was finally published and delivered to his house just weeks before his death in 1931. Bentley was pleased. He never made more than a few thousand dollars from his work, but it had been a labor of love and he was satisfied to know that he would finally be able to share the beauty of his snow crystals with the world.

During the Discussion: As you and your partner discuss each question, take notes on how your partner's ideas either differ from or build upon your own.

Discussion Questions	Other Ideas Expressed	Comparison to My Own Ideas
1. What motivated Bentley's life work?		
2. What achievement gave him fulfillment at the end of his life?		

© Pearson Education, Inc. All rights reserved.

Name _____ Date _____

"A Special Gift–The Legacy of 'Snowflake' Bentley" by Barbara Eaglesham
Take Notes for Research

As you research **snow crystals,** you can use the organizer below to take notes from your sources. As necessary, continue your notes on the back of this page, on note cards, or in a word-processing document.

Snow Crystals	
Main Idea _____ _____ **Quotation or Paraphrase** _____ _____ _____ _____ _____ **Source Information** _____ _____ _____ _____	**Main Idea** _____ _____ **Quotation or Paraphrase** _____ _____ _____ _____ _____ **Source Information** _____ _____ _____ _____
Main Idea _____ _____ **Quotation or Paraphrase** _____ _____ _____ _____ _____ **Source Information** _____ _____ _____ _____	**Main Idea** _____ _____ **Quotation or Paraphrase** _____ _____ _____ _____ _____ **Source Information** _____ _____ _____ _____

© Pearson Education, Inc. All rights reserved.

Name _____ Date _____

"A Special Gift–The Legacy of 'Snowflake' Bentley" by Barbara Eaglesham
Take Notes for Writing to Sources

Planning Your Informative Text: Before you begin drafting your **informative text**, use the chart below to organize your ideas. Follow the directions in each section.

---

1. Identify your topic and jot down details to use in writing your introduction.

_____

_____

_____

_____

---

2. List facts, examples, and other details that explain and illustrate your topic. Use science terms when appropriate.

_____

_____

_____

_____

_____

_____

_____

_____

_____

_____

_____

---

3. Jot down notes for your summary. It should include your main idea and most important ideas.

_____

_____

_____

_____

"All Stories Are Anansi's" by Harold Courlander
Vocabulary Builder

Selection Vocabulary

acknowledge   dispute   opinion

A. DIRECTIONS: *Write the letter of the word that means the same or about the same as the vocabulary word. Then use the italicized word in a complete sentence.*

_____ 1. *dispute*

    A. argument   **C.** error

    B. lie   **D.** agreement

_____

_____ 2. *opinion*

    A. statement   **C.** statistic

    B. fact   **D.** belief

_____

_____ 3. *acknowledge*

    A. taunt   **C.** admit

    B. challenge   **D.** dismiss

_____

Academic Vocabulary

communicate   contribute   tradition

B. DIRECTIONS: *Follow each direction. Write complete sentences for your responses.*

1. Describe one way that people can *communicate* besides by talking.

_____

_____

2. Suggest how someone can *contribute* to the community.

_____

_____

3. What is one *tradition* many Americans enjoy on Independence Day?

_____

_____

© Pearson Education, Inc. All rights reserved.

"All Stories Are Anansi's" by Harold Courlander
Take Notes for Discussion

Before the Small Group Discussion: Read the following passage from the selection.

The Sky God said: "I am willing to sell the stories, but the price is high. Many people have come to me offering to buy, but the price was too high for them. Rich and powerful families have not been able to pay. Do you think you can do it?"

Anansi replied to the Sky God: "I can do it. What is the price?"

During the Discussion: As the group discusses each question, take notes on how other students' ideas either differ from or build upon your own.

Discussion Questions	Other Ideas Expressed	Comparison to My Own Ideas
1. What does the rich and powerful families' inability to pay suggest about the price?		
2. Why does Anansi say he can do it before he knows the Sky God's price?		

© Pearson Education, Inc. All rights reserved.

Name _____ Date _____

"All Stories Are Anansi's" by Harold Courlander
Take Notes for Research

As you research **a trickster character,** use the forms below to take notes from your sources. As necessary, continue your notes on the back of this page, on note cards, or in a word-processing document.

Source Information   Check one: ☐ Primary Source   ☐ Secondary Source

Title: _____   Author: _____

Publication Information: _____

Page(s): _____

Main Idea: _____

_____

Quotation or Paraphrase: _____

_____

Source Information   Check one: ☐ Primary Source   ☐ Secondary Source

Title: _____   Author: _____

Publication Information: _____

Page(s): _____

Main Idea: _____

_____

Quotation or Paraphrase: _____

_____

Source Information   Check one: ☐ Primary Source   ☐ Secondary Source

Title: _____   Author: _____

Publication Information: _____

Page(s): _____

Main Idea: _____

_____

Quotation or Paraphrase: _____

_____

Name _____ Date _____

"All Stories Are Anansi's" by Harold Courlander
Take Notes for Writing to Sources

Planning Your Narrative: Before you begin drafting your **fictional narrative,** use the chart below to organize your ideas. First, identify the character whose point of view you will use. Then follow the directions at the top of each section of the chart.

Character: _____

1. Introduce the characters and setting. Explain the trickster's motivation.

_____

_____

_____

_____

2. List the main plot events for the story. Think about events that would benefit from vivid description using strong sensory details.

_____

_____

_____

_____

_____

_____

_____

_____

_____

_____

3. Plan the conclusion of the narrative. It should follow from, and reflect back upon, the series of events. Tell whether or not the trickster got what he or she wanted.

_____

_____

_____

_____

© Pearson Education, Inc. All rights reserved.

Maslow's Theory of Motivation and Human Needs
Vocabulary Builder and Take Notes for Research

Academic Vocabulary

assumption   culture   explain

DIRECTIONS: *Write the letter of the word that means the <u>opposite</u> of the vocabulary word. Then, use the vocabulary word in a sentence.*

_____ 1. ASSUMPTION

         A. belief   C. hope

         B. doubt   D. illness

_____

_____ 2. CULTURE

         A. sophistication   C. social events

         B. biology   D. unsophistication

_____

_____ 3. EXPLAIN

         A. confuse   C. repeat

         B. analyze   D. clarify

_____

Take Notes for Research

As you research **Abraham Maslow's ideas** for your informal speech or presentation, you can take notes in the forms below. As necessary, continue your notes on the back of this page, on note cards, or in a word-processing document.

Source Information Check one: ☐ Primary Source ☐ Secondary Source	
Title: _____	Author: _____
Publication Information: _____	
Page(s): _____	
Main Idea: _____	
_____	
Quotation or Paraphrase: _____	
_____	

© Pearson Education, Inc. All rights reserved.

Unit 3: Poetry
Big Question Vocabulary—1

The Big Question: What is the best way to communicate?

communicate: *v.* to exchange information with others; other forms: *communication, communicating, communicated*

elaborate: *v.* to give more details or information about a topic

       adj. having a lot of small parts or details put together in a complicated way; other forms: elaborated, elaborating, elaboration

entertain: *v.* to amuse or interest others in a way that makes them happy; other forms: *entertainment, entertaining, entertained*

generate: *v.* to create or develop new ideas on a topic; other forms: *generated, generator*

listen: *v.* to pay attention to what someone is saying; other forms: *listening, listened, listener*

A. DIRECTIONS: *Read each sentence carefully. Each one describes an action that is the* **opposite** *of the action that a vocabulary word describes. Identify each vocabulary word. Write it on the line following the word* **Opposite**.

Example: He wanted to *open* the door. Opposite:_____shut_____	

1. I decided to *ignore* what he said.   **Opposite:** _____

2. Let's *simplify* this complicated issue.   **Opposite:** _____

3. He will bore the audience with that performance.   **Opposite:** _____

4. She wanted to *conceal* her ideas.   **Opposite:** _____

5. He wanted us to *use his old plans and ideas*.   **Opposite:** _____

B. DIRECTIONS: *Complete each sentence by adding the correct vocabulary word.*

1. The school principal asked the students to _____ new ideas about improving school safety.

2. If you don't _____ carefully, you won't hear the beautiful, soft call of the Baltimore oriole.

3. I didn't understand the math problem, so I asked the teacher to _____ on the directions.

4. To _____ with each other effectively, you must speak clearly and listen carefully.

5. Using rich, vivid words and humorous situations will help you to _____ your readers.

© Pearson Education, Inc. All rights reserved.

Name _____ Date _____

Unit 3: Poetry
Big Question Vocabulary—2

The Big Question: What is the best way to communicate?

contribute: *v.* to share or give something of value to others; other form: *contribution*

express: *v.* to use words or actions to show thoughts and feelings; other forms: *expression, expressing, expressed*

learn: *v.* to gain knowledge and understanding of information; other forms: *learning, learned*

produce: *v.* to create something; other forms: *production, producing, produced, producer*

teach: *v.* to help someone learn by giving them information; other forms: *teacher, taught*

DIRECTIONS: *List three things as instructed. Then, use the vocabulary word in a sentences about one of the things. You may use one of its other forms, as shown above.*

1. List three ways that a person might use to *express* happiness.

   _____   _____   _____

   Sentence: _____

2. List three things that grandparents and other older people can *teach* young people.

   _____   _____   _____

   Sentence: _____

3. List three things that a person might *produce* with a pencil and paper.

   _____   _____   _____

   Sentence: _____

4. List three ways that a person might *contribute* to his or her neighborhood or community.

   _____   _____   _____

   Sentence: _____

5. List three things that you consider to be the most important things for a young child to *learn*.

   _____   _____   _____

   Sentence: _____

© Pearson Education, Inc. All rights reserved.

Unit 3: Poetry
Big Question Vocabulary—3

The Big Question: What is the best way to communicate?

enrich: *v.* to improve the quality of something; other forms: *enrichment, enriching, enriched*

inform: *v.* to share facts or information with someone; other forms: *information, informed*

media: *n.* institutions or items that present news and other information, including newspapers, magazines, television programs, and Internet sources; other form: *medium*

technology: *n.* machines and equipment that are based on modern knowledge about science; other forms: *technological, technologies*

transmit: *v.* to send a message or signal, through such sources as radios, televisions, or the Internet; other forms: *transmission, transmitting, transmitted*

A. DIRECTIONS: *Give an example of each of the following.*

1. a *technology* that you use at school: _____

2. something that you *transmitted* to someone electronically: _____

3. a way to *enrich* a friendship: _____

4. a fact that you'd like to *inform* people about: _____

5. a specific form of the *media* that you respect as a news source: _____

B. DIRECTIONS: *Imagine that you are a scientist who just discovered life on another planet. On the lines below, write a summary of your findings, telling how you made your discovery, what messages the people sent to you and how they sent them, and why you feel your discovery might improve life on Earth. Use each of the vocabulary words.*

_____

_____

_____

_____

_____

_____

_____

_____

All-in-One Workbok
© Pearson Education, Inc. All rights reserved.
119

Unit 3: Poetry
Applying the Big Question

What is the best way to communicate?

DIRECTIONS: *Complete the chart below to apply what you have learned about communication. One row has been completed for you.*

Example	Type of communica-tion	Purpose	Pros	Cons	What I learned
From Literature	Writing about meaningful family lessons.	To share an important life lesson.	Conveys a personal story to a broader audience.	The audience for poetry is smaller than for media, such as TV.	A metaphor's lesson can apply to many people.
From Literature					
From Science					
From Social Studies					
From Real Life					

© Pearson Education, Inc. All rights reserved.

"Winter" by Nikki Giovanni, **"The Rider"** by Naomi Shihab Nye,
"Seal" by William Jay Smith, **Haiku** by Bashō

Writing About the Big Question

What is the best way to communicate?

Big Question Vocabulary

communicate	contribute	enrich	entertain	express
inform	learn	listen	media	produce
react	speak	teach	technology	transmit

A. *Use one or more words from the list above to complete each sentence.*

1. Helping others to _____ new skills is a good way to communicate.

2. One way to communicate what you know is to _____ a skill to someone else.

3. When you _____ your knowledge to others, they find out about you as well as your subject.

4. You can use _____ such as computers to communicate your knowledge.

B. *Answer each question with a complete sentence.*

1. Write down two things you have taught another person. Use at least two of the Big Question vocabulary words.

   _____

   _____

2. Write two sentences explaining how you communicated the knowledge you taught.

   _____

   _____

C. *In "Poetry Collection 1," four poets use different forms to share their thoughts or observations. Complete these sentences:*

Through poetry, writers **communicate** _____.

I most enjoy reading poems that **express** _____.

All-in-One Workbook
© Pearson Education, Inc. All rights reserved.
121

Name _____ Date _____

Poetry Collection: Nikki Giovanni, Naomi Shihab Nye, William Jay Smith, Bashō

Reading: Draw Conclusions

Drawing conclusions means arriving at an overall judgment or idea by pulling together several details. By drawing conclusions, you recognize meanings that are not directly stated. **Asking questions** can help you identify details and make connections that lead to a conclusion. You might ask yourself questions such as these:

- What details does the writer include and emphasize?
- How are the details related?
- What do the details mean all together?

Consider, for example, this haiku by Bashō:

On sweet plum blossoms

The sun rises suddenly.

Look, a mountain path!

What do the details suggest? The sun suddenly rises and shines on "sweet plum blossoms," so the setting must be outdoors at dawn. Why, though, does the speaker excitedly point out "a mountain path"? We might conclude that the speaker is gazing at the blossoms when he or she suddenly sees the path ahead. We might also conclude that the speaker is excited to follow the path.

DIRECTIONS: *Complete the following chart. First, ask a question about the poem. Then, record the details that prompted the question. Finally, write a conclusion that you can draw based on the question and the related details.*

Poem	Question	Details Relating to Question	Conclusion
"The Rider"			
"Seal"			
"Winter"			
"Temple bells die out."			

Name _____ Date _____

Poetry Collection: Nikki Giovanni, Naomi Shihab Nye, William Jay Smith, Bashō

Literary Analysis: Forms of Poetry

There are many different **forms of poetry.** A poet will follow different rules depending on the structure of a poem. These are the three forms represented by the poems in this collection:

- A **lyric poem** expresses the poet's thoughts and feelings about a single image or idea in vivid, musical language.
- In a **concrete poem,** the poet arranges the letters and lines to create a visual image that suggests the poem's subject.
- **Haiku** is a traditional form of Japanese poetry that is often about nature. In a traditional haiku, the first line always has five syllables, the second line always has seven syllables, and the third line always has five syllables.

DIRECTIONS: *Write your responses to the following questions.*

1. If you were to rewrite "The Rider" as a concrete poem, what shape would you use to express the main idea of the poem? Why?

   _____

   _____

2. If you were to rewrite "Seal" as a haiku, what seven-syllable line might you write that contained the phrase "Quicksilver-quick"?

   _____

3. If you were to rewrite one of Bashō's haiku as a lyric poem, on what single image would you focus? Why?

   _____

   _____

4. If you were to rewrite "Winter" as a haiku, what seven-syllable line might you write that contained the phrase "Bears store fat"?

   _____

5. If you were to rewrite "Seal" as a lyric poem, how would you change it? Why?

   _____

   _____

Poetry Collection: Nikki Giovanni, Naomi Shihab Nye, William Jay Smith, Bashō
Vocabulary Builder

Word List

fragrant   luminous   minnow   swerve   translates   utter

A. DIRECTIONS: *Provide an explanation for your answer to each question.*

1. Would you be able to see *luminous* stars in a clear night sky?

   _____

   _____

2. If someone did not *utter* a word, would she be likely to win a debate?

   _____

   _____

3. Which would you describe as *fragrant*, vegetables rotting or bread baking?

   _____

   _____

4. Would a driver likely go into a *swerve* to avoid hitting something in the road?

   _____

   _____

5. Would you find a *minnow* in a forest?

   _____

   _____

6. Imagine a poem that is written in a language that you cannot read. If someone *translates* that poem into English, could you read it?

   _____

   _____

B. WORD STUDY: *The Latin root -lum- means "light." Write a sentence that answers each question, using the italicized word.*

1. If a soccer field is *illuminated*, what time of day is the game probably being played?

   _____

2. What part of the ocean is a *bioluminescent* fish likely to live in?

   _____

3. If someone is a *luminary* in the field of medicine, what do people probably think of the person?

   _____

© Pearson Education, Inc. All rights reserved.

Poetry Collection: Nikki Giovanni, Naomi Shihab Nye, William Jay Smith, Bashō

Conventions: Sentence Functions and Endmarks

Sentences are classified into four categories, according to their function.

Category, Function, and Endmark	Example
A **declarative sentence** makes a statement. It ends with a period. (.)	This is a beautiful poem.
An **interrogative sentence** asks a question. It ends with a question mark. (?)	Who wrote this poem?
An **imperative sentence** gives a command. It ends with a period or an exclamation point. (. or !)	Remind me of that poet's name. Hurry up and tell me her name!
An **exclamatory sentence** calls out or exclaims. It ends with an exclamation point. (!)	Oh, I know! Her name is Nikki Giovanni!

Note that the subject of an imperative sentence is always the word *you*, and it is never stated: *(You) remind me of that poet's name. (You) hurry up!*

Also note that in your writing, you should use exclamatory sentences as if they were a powerful spice. For the greatest effect, use them sparingly (not very often).

A. DIRECTIONS: *Add the correct endmark to each sentence. Then, identify the sentence as* declarative, interrogative, imperative, *or* exclamatory.

1. What kind of poem do you want to write _____ _____

2. I want to write a few haiku _____ _____

3. Hey, that rhymes _____ _____

4. The vowel sound in *few* rhymes with the second vowel sound in
   haiku _____ _____

5. Think of another word that rhymes with *few* _____ _____

6. Well, *true* rhymes with *few*, and so does *kangaroo* _____ _____

7. Doesn't all this rhyming make you want to write a poem that
   rhymes _____ _____

B. Writing Application: *Write a short dialogue between two characters. Use at least one of each kind of sentence. Label your sentences* dec *for declarative,* int *for interrogative,* imp *for imperative, and* exclam *for exclamatory.*

_____

_____

_____

_____

© Pearson Education, Inc. All rights reserved.

Name _____ Date _____

Support for Writing to Sources: Lyric Poem, Concrete Poem, or Haiku

In the chart below, write details that you might use in your poem.

Subject: _____

Vivid Descriptions	Action Words	Thoughts	Feelings

Now, use the details you have collected to draft a **lyric poem, concrete poem,** or **haiku.**

© Pearson Education, Inc. All rights reserved.

Poetry Collection: Nikki Giovanni, Naomi Shihab Nye, William Jay Smith, Bashō

Support for Listening and Speaking: Presentation

With the other members of your group, choose a recording of a poet reading his or her lyric poems. Before you listen to the poems, write down the name of the poet and the names of the poems you plan to listen to. Then, as you listen or just after you finish listening, record your opinion of each poem, and list two reasons for your opinion. You might want to listen to the recording several times. Finally, use your notes to deliver a brief **presentation** to your group in which you express your opinion of the reading and cite the reasons for your opinion.

Poet: _____

Poems: _____

_____

My opinion: _____

_____

_____

_____

Reason 1: _____

_____

_____

_____

Reason 2: _____

_____

_____

_____

© Pearson Education, Inc. All rights reserved.

"Life" by Naomi Long Madgett, **"The Courage that My Mother Had"** by Edna St. Vincent Millay, **"Mother to Son"** by Langston Hughes, **"Fog"** by Carl Sandburg

Writing About the Big Question

What is the best way to communicate?

Big Question Vocabulary

communicate	contribute	enrich	entertain	express
inform	learn	listen	media	produce
react	speak	teach	technology	transmit

A. *Use one or more words from the list above to complete each sentence.*

1. The _____, such as newspapers and television, is a useful way to communicate.

2. News articles can _____ you about important events and issues.

3. Stories about other cultures can _____ your understanding about how others live.

4. Reading and listening to the news can _____ a greater understanding of the world.

B. *Answer each question with a complete sentence.*

1. Write two things you have learned about other cultures from newspapers or television. Use two Big Question vocabulary words in your response.

   _____

   _____

2. Explain how your knowledge of other cultures has helped you understand the world more fully. Use two Big Question vocabulary words in your response.

   _____

   _____

C. *In Poetry Collection 2, each poem includes one or more comparisons between objects or ideas. Complete this sentence:*

When you make connections between unrelated things, you **enrich**

_____ and **learn** _____.

© Pearson Education, Inc. All rights reserved.

Poetry Collection: Naomi Long Madgett, Edna St. Vincent Millay,
Langston Hughes, Carl Sandburg

Reading: Draw Conclusions

A **conclusion** is a decision or an opinion that you reach after considering the details in a literary work. **Connecting the details** can help you draw conclusions as you read. For example, if the speaker in a poem uses the words *tacks, splinters, boards, bare,* and *dark,* you might conclude that he or she wishes to create an image of hardship. As you read, identify important details. Then, look at the details together and draw a conclusion about the poem or the speaker.

DIRECTIONS: *In the first column of the chart below are details from the poems in this collection. Consider each set of details, and use them to draw a conclusion about the poem. Write your conclusion in the second column.*

Details	Conclusion
"Life": • The speaker says that life is a toy. • The toy ticks for a while, amusing an infant. • The toy, a watch, stops running.	
"Mother to Son": • The speaker describes the staircase she has climbed: it has tacks, splinters, bare boards, and places with no light. • The speaker is still climbing.	
"The Courage That My Mother Had": • The speaker's mother had courage. • The speaker has a brooch her mother wore. • The speaker wants her mother's courage.	
"Fog": • The fog arrives "on little cat feet." • The fog sits "on silent haunches." • The fog looks "over harbor and city / . . . and then moves on."	

© Pearson Education, Inc. All rights reserved.

Name _____ Date _____

Poetry Collection: Naomi Long Madgett, Edna St. Vincent Millay,
Langston Hughes, Carl Sandburg

Literary Analysis: Figurative Language

Figurative language is language that is not meant to be taken literally. Writers use figures of speech to express ideas in vivid and imaginative ways. Common figures of speech include the following:

- A **simile** compares two unlike things using a word such as *like* or *as*.
- A **metaphor** compares two unlike things by stating that one thing is another thing. In an **extended metaphor,** several related comparisons extend over a number of lines.
- **Personification** gives human characteristics to a nonhuman subject.
- A **symbol** is an object, a person, an animal, a place, or an image that represents something else.

Look at this line from "Life." What figure of speech does the poet use?

Life is but a toy that swings on a bright gold chain.

The speaker uses a metaphor to compare life to a toy.

DIRECTIONS: *As you read the poems in this collection, record the similes, metaphors, extended metaphors, personification, and symbols.*

Poem	Passage	Figurative Language
"Life"		
"Mother to Son"		
"The Courage That My Mother Had"		
"Fog"		

Poetry Collection: Naomi Long Madgett, Edna St. Vincent Millay,
Langston Hughes, Carl Sandburg
Vocabulary Builder

Word List

    crystal   fascinated   granite   haunches

A. DIRECTIONS: *Read each sentence, paying attention to the italicized word. Then, explain whether the sentence makes sense. If it does not make sense, rewrite the sentence or write a new sentence, using the italicized word correctly.*

1. The cheetah sprang from its *haunches* to bring down the fleeing antelope.

   Explanation: _____

   New sentence: _____

2. The *crystal* vase shattered when it hit the ground.

   Explanation: _____

   New sentence: _____

3. Anita was so *fascinated* by the movie that she fell asleep.

   Explanation: _____

   New Sentence: _____

4. The piece of *granite* dissolved in the hard rain.

   Explanation: _____

   New Sentence: _____

B. WORD STUDY: *The suffix -er means "one who." Answer each question or pair of questions, using the italicized word with the suffix added.*

1. If you worked in a *bank,* what would some of your duties be?

   _____

2. Would you like to *teach* a classroom full of students your age? Why or why not?

   _____

3. Do you think it is dangerous for people to *climb* tall, icy mountains? Why or why not?

   _____

4. Do you think people find it easy to *write* books? Explain why you think so.

   _____

Name _____   Date _____

Conventions: Independent and Dependent Clauses

A **clause** is a group of words with its own subject and verb. An **independent clause** expresses a complete thought and can stand alone as a sentence. A **dependent clause** has a subject and a verb, but it does not express a complete thought and cannot stand alone. The following sentence contains both an independent and a dependent clause. The subject in each clause is underlined once, and the verb is underlined twice. The dependent clause appears in italics:

> Langston Hughes was a Harlem Renaissance poet, *though his poetry fits in other categories, as well.*

A dependent clause may appear either before or after the independent clause:

> *Though his poetry fits in other categories, as well,* Langston Hughes was a Harlem Renaissance poet.

There are two kinds of dependent clauses. A **subordinate clause** begins with a subordinating conjunction, such as *if, when because, where,* or *though.* A **relative clause** begins with a relative pronoun, such as *who, whom, which,* or *that.*

A. DIRECTIONS: *In each sentence, underline the independent clause once and the dependent clause twice.*

1. **Naomi Long** Madgett admired the poets Tennyson and Langston Hughes, whose works inspired her.

2. Because Edna St. Vincent Millay's mother was a hard-working nurse, Edna grew up to be independent and successful.

3. Langston Hughes published his first work when he was only one year out of high school.

4. Carl Sandburg, who had worked as a cook, soldier, and stagehand, finally became a famous poet and won two Pulitzer Prizes.

5. Because she is an ambitious, talented writer, Madgett's work had appeared in over ten poetry books by 2006.

B. Writing Application: *Rewrite each sentence by adding a subordinate clause beginning with* though *or* although.

1. Naomi Long Madgett also compares life to a watch.

   _____

2. The speaker in "The Courage That My Mother Had" owns her mother's gold brooch.

   _____

3. The mother in "Mother to Son" is still alive and doing her best.

   _____

4. Fog might also be the color of a pale gray cat.

   _____

© Pearson Education, Inc. All rights reserved.

Name _____ Date _____

Poetry Collection: Naomi Long Madgett, Edna St. Vincent Millay, Langston Hughes, Carl Sandburg

Support for Writing to Sources: Metaphor

Use the word web below to collect ideas for an **extended metaphor** about a quality or an idea, such as love, loyalty, life, or death. Decide on the quality or idea, and then decide what you will compare it to. It may be an object, an animal, or an idea. Write your ideas in the center of the web. Then, complete the web by writing down ideas that relate to your central idea. Use vivid images and descriptive language. Your extended metaphor may include similes, metaphors, personification, and symbols.

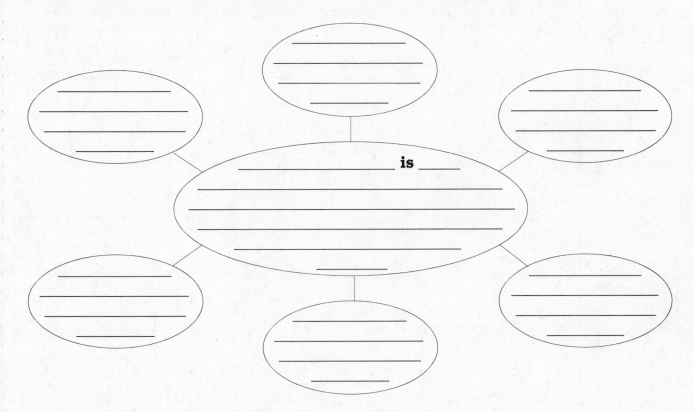

Now, use your notes to write an extended metaphor about a quality or an idea. Be sure to use vivid images and descriptive language.

Name _____ Date _____

Support for Research and Technology: Scientific Explanation

With a partner, decide how you will divide up the research you need to do to find differences between fog and smog. Then, use this chart to record your findings. In the column headed **Visual Aids**, make notes about Venn diagrams, comparison charts, photographs, and/or diagrams you might use in your presentation.

	Fog	**Smog**	**Visual Aids**
Definition			
Similarities			
Differences			
Types			

© Pearson Education, Inc. All rights reserved.

"Full Fathom Five" by William Shakespeare, **"Onomatopoeia"** by Eve Merriam,
"Train Tune" by Louise Bogan, **"Sarah Cynthia Sylvia Stout Would
Not Take the Garbage Out"** by Shel Silverstein

Writing About the Big Question
What is the best way to communicate?

Big Question Vocabulary

communicate	contribute	enrich	entertain	express
inform	learn	listen	media	produce
react	speak	teach	technology	transmit

A. *Use one or more words from the list above to complete each sentence.*

1. When you have a problem with a friend, you can _____ your opinion by talking it over.

2. It is important to _____ to your friend's opinions, too.

3. Listening well and speaking honestly can _____ a friendship.

B. *Answer each question with a complete sentence.*

1. Describe two occasions when you have expressed an opinion to a friend. Use two of the Big Question vocabulary words.

   _____

   _____

2. Choose one of the discussions above. Explain how the discussion helped to enrich your friendship.

   _____

   _____

C. *In "Poetry Collection 3," each poem uses sound to create an image or to bring about a certain mood. Complete this sentence:*

When you really **listen**, you can _____.

Poetry Collection: William Shakespeare, Eve Merriam, Louise Bogan, Shel Silverstein

Reading: Paraphrase

When you **paraphrase,** you restate something in your own words. To paraphrase a poem, you must first understand it. **Reading aloud according to punctuation** can help you identify complete thoughts in a poem and therefore grasp its meaning. Because poets do not always complete a sentence at the end of a line, pausing simply because a line ends can interfere with your understanding of the meaning. Follow these rules when you read aloud:

- Keep reading when a line has no end punctuation.
- Pause at commas, dashes, and semicolons.
- Stop at end marks, such as periods, question marks, or exclamation points.

As you read poetry, allow the punctuation to help you paraphrase the poet's ideas.

DIRECTIONS: *The following quotations are from the poems in this collection. Read each item aloud, following the rules above. Then, paraphrase the lines. That is, restate them in your own words.*

1. spurts,
   finally stops sputtering
   and plash!
   gushes rushes splashes
   clear water dashes.

   _____

   _____

2. Back through lightning
   Back through cities
   Back through stars
   Back through hours

   _____

   _____

3. Sea nymphs hourly ring his knell;
   Ding-dong.
   Hark! Now I hear them ding-dong bell.

   _____

   _____

4. Poor Sarah met an awful fate,
   That I cannot right now relate
   Because the hour is much too late.

   _____

   _____

© Pearson Education, Inc. All rights reserved.

Name _____ Date _____

Poetry Collection: William Shakespeare, Eve Merriam, Louise Bogan, Shel Silverstein
Literary Analysis: Sound Devices

Sound devices create musical effects that appeal to the ear. Here are some common sound devices used in poetry:

- **Onomatopoeia** is the use of words whose sounds suggest their meaning:

The saw cut through the tree with a <u>buzz</u>. The librarian <u>murmured</u> her answer.

- **Alliteration** is the repetition of sounds at the beginnings of words:

<u>P</u>eter <u>P</u>iper <u>p</u>icked a <u>p</u>eck of <u>p</u>ickled <u>p</u>eppers.

- **Repetition** is the repeated use of words, phrases, and/or rhythms:

<u>The leaves blew</u> up, / <u>The leaves blew</u> down, / <u>The leaves blew</u> all around the town.

In the last example, there is repetition of both the words (*The leaves blew*) and the rhythm. In poetry, a line may contain more than one sound device.

DIRECTIONS: *The following quotations are from the poems in this collection. Read each item, and decide which sound device or devices the lines contain. Identify the sound device or devices by writing* Onomatopoeia, Alliteration, *and/or* Repetition.

1. Full fathom five thy father lies

    _____

2. The rusty spigot
   sputters,
   utters
   a splutter

    _____

3. Back through clouds
   Back through clearing
   Back through distance
   Back through silence

    _____

4. finally stops sputtering
   and plash!
   gushes rushes splashes
   clear water dashes

    _____

5. Crusts of black burned buttered toast.

    _____

Poetry Collection: William Shakespeare, Eve Merriam, Louise Bogan, Shel Silverstein
Vocabulary Builder

Word List
curdled   fathom   groves   smattering   sputters   withered

A. DIRECTIONS: *Read each item, and think about the meaning of the italicized word from the Word List. Then, answer the question, and explain your answer.*

1. The milk has *curdled* in the bottle. Would you drink it?

   _____

2. If a person *sputters* as she speaks, is she likely to be calm?

   _____

3. If there are orange *groves* on your property, are there trees on your property?

   _____

4. If you are measuring the depths of a lake, would you measure in *fathoms*?

   _____

5. If you were hit by a *smattering* of raindrops, would you need to change your clothes?

   _____

6. The *withered* flowers had been in the vase for a week. They are now brightly colored?

   _____

B. WORD STUDY: *The Latin suffix -less means "without." Decide whether each statement is true or false. Write T or F. Then, explain your answer.*

1. You could trust someone who is *careless* with your most prized possession.

   T / F: _____ **Explanation:** _____

2. A movie that seems *endless* is very long or very dull.

   T / F: _____ **Explanation:** _____

3. A *joyless* person is almost always happy.

   T / F: _____ **Explanation:** _____

   _____

© Pearson Education, Inc. All rights reserved.

Poetry Collection: Louise Bogan, William Shakespeare, Shel Silverstein, Eve Merriam

Conventions: Sentence Structures

A **simple sentence** is an independent clause. That is, it is a group of words that has a subject and a verb and can stand by itself as a complete thought.

A **compound sentence** consists of two or more independent clauses that are joined by a conjunction such as *and, but, or,* or *for.*

Shakespeare is most famous for the plays he wrote, <u>but</u> he also wrote poems.

A **complex sentence** contains one independent clause and one or more dependent clauses. In this sentence, the dependent clause is underlined:

<u>Besides being an amazing playwright</u>, Shakespeare was a gifted poet.

A **compound-complex sentence** contains two or more independent clauses and one or more dependent clauses. In this sentence, the independent clauses are underlined once, and the dependent clause, twice.

<u>Shakespeare's comedies</u>, <u>of which there are seventeen</u>, <u>amused audiences in his time</u>, and <u>they continue to do so today</u>.

A. DIRECTIONS: *Identify each sentence below by writing* Simple, Compound, Complex, *or* Compound-Complex.

1. Poet Louise Bogan was a shy person, and she felt awkward in the public spotlight. _____

2. Although his tragedies are probably more famous, Shakespeare wrote many histories, too. _____

3. Eve Merriam was born in 1916. _____

4. Shakespeare's plays have been translated into every major language. _____

5. Shel Silverstein was a well-known comic poet, but he also did other creative work, which included singing folk songs, composing music, and cartooning. _____

B. Writing Application: *Write a short paragraph in which you describe your reaction to one of the poems in this collection. Tell what you liked most about the poem and why it appeals to you. Use at least one simple sentence, one compound sentence, and one complex sentence. Label your sentences by writing* Simple, Compound, *or* Complex *in parentheses after each one.*

_____

_____

_____

_____

_____

© Pearson Education, Inc. All rights reserved.

Poetry Collection: Louise Bogan, William Shakespeare, Shel Silverstein, Eve Merriam

Support for Writing to Sources: Paraphrase

Use these charts to draft a **paraphrase** of one of the four poems you have read. In the first chart, write down unfamiliar words from the poem, their dictionary definition, and the definition restated in your own words. In the second chart, write each line of the poem in the first column. In the second column, restate the meaning of the line in your own words. If you want to work on the Silverstein poem, choose a section that is eighteen lines long, or shorter, to paraphrase.

Title of poem: _____

Word to Look Up	Dictionary Definition	Definition in My Own Words

Poem, Line by Line	Paraphrase, Line by Line

Now, read over your paraphrase to make sure it has the same meaning as the original. Make your revisions as you prepare your final draft.

Poetry Collection: Shel Silverstein, William Shakespeare, Eve Merriam, Louise Bogan
Support for Speaking and Listening: Poetry Reading

Choose a poem from this collection to present in a **poetry reading.**

Title of poem: _____

Poet's name: _____

Is the tone of the poem serious, humorous, or playful? _____

How might the tone affect the speed at which I read the poem and my tone of voice?

_____

_____

Now, read these guidelines, and decide how they apply to the poem you will read.

• Read the poem aloud. Pause only at commas, dashes, and semicolons. Come to a full stop after periods, question marks, and exclamation points. If there is no punctuation mark at the end of a line, *do not pause.*

• If you are unsure of the meaning of a line, paraphrase it.

• Vary your reading rate.

• Use expression in your voice that is appropriate to the meaning of the lines.

• Practice reading the poem loudly and clearly. Make eye contact with your audience.

"**Jim**" by Gwendolyn Brooks, "**Father William**" by Lewis Carroll,
"**Stopping by Woods on a Snowy Evening**" by Robert Frost,
"**Annabel Lee**" by Edgar Allan Poe

Writing About the Big Question

What is the best way to communicate?

Big Question Vocabulary

communicate	contribute	enrich	entertain	express
inform	learn	listen	media	produce
react	speak	teach	technology	transmit

A. *Use one or more words from the list above to complete each sentence.*

1. When you take part in a poetry slam, you can _____
   an audience with poetry.

2. You _____ yourself through your poetry to the
   audience.

3. Your audience can _____ about you as they
   _____ to your poems.

B. *Answer each question with a complete sentence.*

1. Describe a poem you have listened to or read that you found moving or entertaining.

   _____

   _____

2. Explain why the poem entertained you, and explain what you learned from it. Use at
   least two Big Question vocabulary words in your response.

   _____

   _____

C. *In "Poetry Collection 4," each poem uses rhythm and rhyme to create a musical quality.*
   Complete this sentence:

   Messages that **entertain** as well as **inform** _____.

Poetry Collection: Gwendolyn Brooks, Lewis Carroll, Robert Frost, Edgar Allan Poe

Reading: Paraphrase

To **paraphrase** means to restate or explain something in your own words. When you paraphrase lines of poetry, you make the meaning clear to yourself. If you are unsure of a poem's meaning, **reread** the parts that are difficult. Follow these steps:

- Look up unfamiliar words, and replace them with words you know.
- Restate the line or passage using your own everyday words.
- Reread the passage to make sure that your version makes sense.

Look at these lines from "Father William":

"In my youth," said his father, "I took to the law

    And argued each case with my wife;

And the muscular strength which it gave to my jaw

    Has lasted the rest of my life."

The first line tells you that Father William "took to the law." If you look up *law* in a dictionary, you will learn that one of its meanings is "the legal profession." Father William is saying that he was a lawyer. That knowledge will help you understand the second line: Father William prepared for his legal cases by arguing them with his wife. You probably know or can guess that *muscular* has to do with muscles. Now you have all the ingredients to write a paraphrase of the verse. It might look like this:

"When I was young," Father William said, "I was a lawyer

    And I talked over every case with my wife;

And as a result, I developed strong jaw muscles

    That I still have today."

DIRECTIONS: *Read these passages from "Jim," "Annabel Lee," and "Stopping by Woods on a Snowy Evening." Following the process described above, write a paraphrase of each passage.*

1. The sun should drop its greatest gold / On him.

_____

2. "A wind blew out of a cloud by night / Chilling my Annabel Lee; / So that her highborn kinsmen came / And bore her away from me, / To shut her up in a sepulcher / In this kingdom by the sea."

_____

_____

_____

3. He gives his harness bells a shake / To ask if there is some mistake. / The only other sound's the sweep / Of easy wind and downy flake.

_____

_____

_____

© Pearson Education, Inc. All rights reserved.

Poetry Collection: Gwendolyn Brooks, Lewis Carroll, Robert Frost, Edgar Allan Poe
Literary Analysis: Sound Devices

Sound devices, such as rhythm and rhyme, make poetry musical. **Rhythm** is a poem's pattern of stressed (´) and unstressed (˘) syllables.

Meter is a poem's rhythmical pattern. It is measured in *feet*, or single units of stressed and unstressed syllables. In the examples below, stressed and unstressed syllables are marked, and feet are separated by vertical lines (|). The first line of "Father William" contains four feet, and the second line contains three feet. The two lines of "Stopping by Woods on a Snowy Evening" contain four feet each.

> "You are OLD, | Fa-ther WILL- | iam," the YOUNG | man SAID, |

> And your HAIR | has be-COME | ver-y WHITE" |

Rhyme is the repetition of a sounds at the ends of lines. The two words that rhyme in the lines from "Stopping by Woods on a Snowy Evening" are underlined.

> My LIT- | tle HORSE | must THINK | it QUEER |

> to STOP | with-OUT | a FARM- | house NEAR |

A. DIRECTIONS: *Mark the stressed (´) and unstressed (˘) syllables in these lines. Then, show the meter by drawing a vertical line after each foot.*

1. "You are old," said the youth, "as I mentioned before. / And have grown most

   uncommonly fat."

2. He gives his harness bells a shake / To ask if there is some mistake. / The only

   other sound's the sweep / Of easy wind and downy flake.

B. DIRECTIONS: *Reread the first stanza of Poe's "Annabel Lee." Circle the last word in each line. Then write two sentences to explain which lines rhyme in the stanza.*

It was many and many a year ago,
   In a kingdom by the sea.
That a maiden there lived whom you may know
   By the name of Annabel Lee;—
And this maiden she lived with no other thought
   Than to love and be loved by me.

_____

_____

© Pearson Education, Inc. All rights reserved.

Poetry Collection: Gwendolyn Brooks, Lewis Carroll, Robert Frost, Edgar Allan Poe
Vocabulary Builder

Word List

coveted   downy   envying   incessantly   supple

A. DIRECTIONS: *Read each item, and think about the meaning of the italicized word from the Word List. Then, answer the question, and explain your answer.*

1. Father William stands on his head *incessantly*. Does he stand on his head for an hour at a time, taking breaks when he gets tired?

   _____

2. The speaker in "Annabel Lee" says that the angels *coveted* the love between him and Annabel Lee. Did the angels criticize their love?

   _____

3. Father William used an ointment to keep his joints *supple*. Was he likely to have had trouble bending down to tie his shoes?

   _____

4. The snow falls in *downy* flakes. Is the snow heavy?

   _____

5. The speaker in "Annabel Lee" says the angels were *envying* the love he and Annabel shared. Did the angels want love for themselves?

   _____

B. WORD STUDY: *The Latin prefix* un- *means "not." Answer each question by adding* un- *to each italicized word and using the new word in your response.*

1. What would happen if you were not *prepared* for a test?

   _____

2. Is a fantasy movie likely to have only *realistic* characters?

   _____

3. Is it hard to sleep in a *comfortable* bed?

   _____

© Pearson Education, Inc. All rights reserved.

Poetry Collection: Gwendolyn Brooks, Lewis Carroll, Robert Frost, Edgar Allan Poe
Subject-Verb Agreement

A verb must agree with its subject in **number.**

Singular Subject and Verb: A *battery comes* with the music player.

Plural Subject and Verb: Two *batteries come* with the music player.

Two or more subjects joined by *and* are plural in number and require a plural verb:

Plural Subject and Verb: Two *batteries and* a *plug come* with the music player.

Subjects joined by *or* and *nor* are considered singular unless the *last* part is plural.

Singular Subject and Verb: Either a *battery or* a *plug comes* with the music player.

Singular Subject and Verb: Either two *batteries or* a *plug comes* with the music player.

Plural Subject and Verb: Either a *plug or* two *batteries come* with the music player.

Identifying Correct Subject-Verb Agreement

A. DIRECTIONS: *Complete each sentence by circling the verb that agrees with the subject.*

1. Hot peppers and tomatoes (combines, combine) for a tasty hot sauce.
2. Supermarkets or smaller Mexican groceries (sells, sell) many varieties.
3. Neither my mom nor my sisters (likes, like) my favorite sauce.
4. Either Baton Rouge or New Orleans (produces, produce) a special hot sauce.
5. Two small bottles or a bigger jar (is, are) on my shopping list.

Fixing Incorrect Subject-Verb Agreement

B. DIRECTIONS: *On the lines provided, rewrite these sentences so that they use correct subject-verb agreement. If a sentence is correct as presented, write* correct.

1. Milk and cheese often comes from Wisconsin and Vermont.

   _____

2. Neither Wisconsin nor Vermont produce as much beef as Texas.

   _____

3. Either Brazil or Argentina are known for beef.

   _____

4. Neither Australia nor the British Isles has as many cows as Canada.

   _____

   _____

Name _____   Date _____

Writing to Sources: Poem

Use the following chart to gather details and your thoughts about the poem you will write about a person you know.

My poem is about: _____

Notes About "Annabel Lee"	Notes About "Father William"
_____	_____
_____	_____
_____	_____
_____	_____
_____	_____
_____	_____

Notes About "Jim"	Notes About "Stopping by Woods on a Snowy Evening"
_____	_____
_____	_____
_____	_____
_____	_____
_____	_____
_____	_____

Qualities That Describe My Subject	My Feelings About My Subject
_____	_____
_____	_____
_____	_____
_____	_____
_____	_____
_____	_____
_____	_____
_____	_____

© Pearson Education, Inc. All rights reserved.

Name _____ Date _____

Support for Research and Technology: Survey

As you gather information for your **survey,** use tally marks to enter the results. (With tally marks, each line stands for one vote. Draw every fifth line diagonally through the four preceding lines: ⃦⃥.) Using tally marks, you can easily count by fives to figure out which poem received the most votes in each category.

Category	"Annabel Lee"	"Father William"	"Jim"	"Stopping by Woods on a Snowy Evening"
Best character description				
Best overall use of language				
Best rhythm				
Best rhyme				
Best meter				

Now, circle the winning tally in each category. Which poem is the winner in the most categories? That poem is the class favorite. Write its title here. (If it's a tie, write both titles.)

Winner of Class-Favorite-Poem Award: _____

Poetry by Walt Whitman and E. E. Cummings
Writing About the Big Question

What is the best way to communicate?

Big Question Vocabulary

communicate	contribute	enrich	entertain	express
inform	learn	listen	media	produce
react	speak	teach	technology	transmit

A. *Use one or more words from the list above to complete each sentence.*

1. You can _____ with others by speaking, writing, or through the arts.

2. All communication helps you _____ about other people.

3. Communication can _____ your life and the lives of others.

B. *Respond to each item with a complete sentence.*

1. Describe your favorite way to communicate and tell when you are likely to use it. Use at least two Big Question vocabulary words.

   _____

   _____

   _____

2. Explain why you prefer to communicate in the way you have chosen. Tell how it helps you express yourself and learn about other people.

   _____

   _____

   _____

C. In the poetry of Whitman and Cummings, the writers use imagery to paint vivid pictures in the minds of readers. Think about the Big Question as you complete the sentence.

Descriptive words can enrich a piece of writing because _____ .

   _____

   _____

   _____

Poetry by Walt Whitman and E. E. Cummings
Literary Analysis: Comparing Imagery

In poetry, an **image** is a word or phrase that appeals to one or more of the five senses. Writers use **imagery** to bring poetry to life with descriptions of how their subjects look, sound, feel, taste, and smell.

Both "Miracles" and "in Just—" contain images that appeal to the senses. For example, "wade with naked feet along the beach" appeals to the sense of touch, and "the little lame balloonman" appeals to sight.

DIRECTIONS: *Read each image in the first column, and mark an X in the column or columns to indicate the sense or senses that the image appeals to. The first fifteen images are from "Miracles"; the last nine are from "in Just—."*

Image	Sight	Hearing	Touch	Taste	Smell
1. "walk the streets of Manhattan"					
2. "dart my sight over the roofs"					
3. "stand under trees in the woods"					
4. "talk by day with any one I love"					
5. "sit at table at dinner with the rest"					
6. "look at strangers opposite me"					
7. "honeybees busy around the hive"					
8. "animals feeding in the fields"					
9. "birds, or . . . insects in the air"					
10. "the sundown"					
11. "stars shining so quiet and bright"					
12. "thin curve of the new moon"					
13. "fishes that swim the rocks"					
14. "the motion of the waves"					
15. "the ships with men in them"					
16. "the world is mud-luscious"					
17. "little lame balloonman whistles"					
18. "eddieandbill come running"					
19. "from marbles and piracies"					
20. "the world is puddle-wonderful"					
21. "queer old balloonman whistles"					
22. "bettyandisbel come dancing"					
23. "from hop-scotch and jump-rope"					

© Pearson Education, Inc. All rights reserved.

Poetry by Walt Whitman and E. E. Cummings
Vocabulary Builder

Word List
distinct   exquisite

A. DIRECTIONS: *Complete these word maps by writing synonyms, antonyms, and an example sentence for each vocabulary word.*

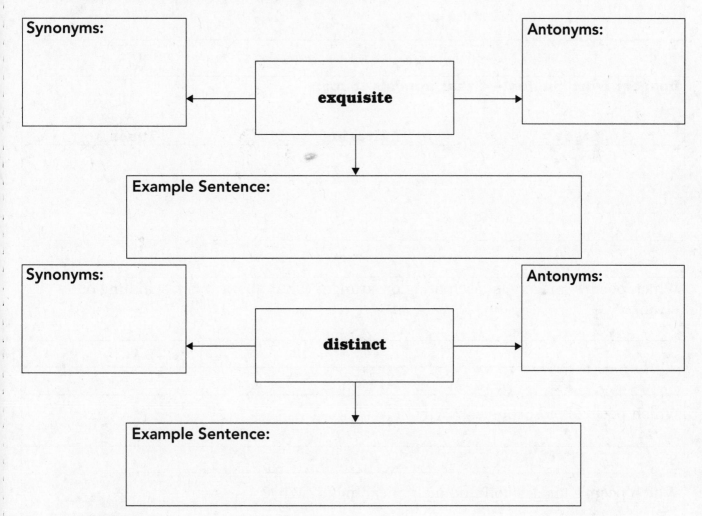

B. DIRECTIONS: *Write the letter of the word or words whose meaning is most nearly the same as the word from the Word List.*

____ 1. exquisite
   A. quaint   **B.** significant   **C.** costly   **D.** beautiful

____ 2. distinct
   A. blurry   **B.** separate   **C.** similar   **D.** pure

© Pearson Education, Inc. All rights reserved.

Name _____ Date _____

Poetry by Walt Whitman and E. E. Cummings
Support for Writing to Compare Literary Works

Use the following graphic organizers as you prepare to write an essay recommending either "Miracles" or "in Just—" to someone your age.

Imagery from "Miracles" that appeals to me:

Sight	Hearing	Touch

Imagery from "in Just—" that appeals to me:

Sight	Hearing	Touch

Which poem's imagery is fascinating or strange? What about it is fascinating or strange?

_____

_____

Which poem is more musical? Why?

_____

_____

Which poem's images do I find more meaningful? Why?

_____

_____

_____

Now, use your notes to write an essay about the poem that you would recommend.

Name _____   Date _____

Comparison-and-Contrast Essay

Prewriting: Gathering Details

Use the following Venn diagram to organize the details of your comparison-and-contrast essay. Fill in details about one subject on the left side of the diagram and details about the other on the right side. Use the middle for details the subjects share.

Subject 1: _____   **Subject 2:** _____

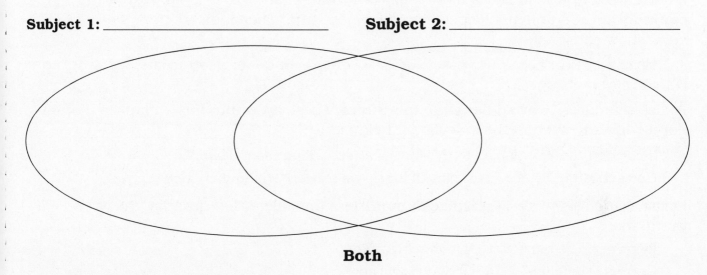

Both

Drafting: Using the SEE Method

Use this graphic organizer to develop your comparison-and-contrast essay.

State the main idea in every paragraph to make sure you stay on topic. Write your main ideas in this column:

Main Ideas	*Extend* your thoughts with specific examples that prove your main ideas:	*Elaborate* by providing further details to describe your examples:
Paragraph 1:		
Paragraph 2:		
Paragraph 3:		
Paragraph 4:		
Paragraph 5:		

© Pearson Education, Inc. All rights reserved.

Name _____ Date _____

Writer's Toolbox

Sentence Fluency: Revising Sentence Structures to Clarify Relationships

If clauses in a sentence are equally important, use **coordinating conjunctions**. Often, using the conjunctions *or, but,* or *so* makes the relationship between clauses clearer than using *and* does:

It was cold, ~~and we~~ *so we* wore our warm coats.

If one clause in a sentence is more important than another, use a **subordinating conjunction**. Conjunctions such as *after, before,* and *when* indicate time; *because* or *since* show cause-effect:

When we fell asleep, it was past midnight. *Because* we got to sleep so late, we slept late the next morning.

Revise sentences to avoid **dangling modifiers**. These are subordinate clauses that do not modify any word in the independent clause:

Incorrect: After beginning to think, we started writing them down.

Correct: After we began to think of ideas, we started writing them down.

Revise sentences to avoid **misplaced modifiers** (modifiers that describe the wrong word), too:

Incorrect: The girl is smiling in the red jacket.

Correct: The girl in the red jacket is smiling.

Revising Sentences to Clarify Coordination and Subordination

A. DIRECTIONS: *Circle the conjunction that combines the two clauses into one sentence by best expressing the relationship between the clauses.*

1. Whole-grain bread tastes good, (and, or, but, so) most brands are very healthy.
2. Grandma cannot eat salty foods, (and, or, but, so) Dad bought her some low-salt crackers.
3. (After, Since) we got home, we ate some spinach lasagna with red bell pepper sauce.
4. (Before, Because) your body needs rest, try to get eight to ten hours of sleep each night.

Revising Sentences to Avoid Dangling and Misplaced Modifiers

B. DIRECTIONS: *Rewrite each sentence to correct a dangling or misplaced modifier.*

1. After cooking over a low flame for an hour, Mom poured it over some whole-grain pasta.

   _____

2. That boy is the one we came to meet in the red sweatshirt.

   _____

3. When you have washed and dried, you can cut them up and put them in the salad bowl.

   _____

4. Someone was laughing really loudly in the audience.

   _____

"The Highwayman" by Alfred Noyes
Vocabulary Builder

Selection Vocabulary

bound   strove   torrent

A. DIRECTIONS: *Decide whether each statement below is true or false. On the line before each item, write TRUE or FALSE. Then explain your answers.*

_____   1. Wind picked up the dust from the dry *torrent* of the river.

_____.

_____   2. Megan *bound* her dog to a post while she went into the store.

_____.

_____   3. The runner *strove* to reach the finish line first.

_____.

Academic Vocabulary

contrast   identify   opposing

B. DIRECTIONS: *Complete each sentence with a word, phrase, or clause that contains a context clue for the italicized word.*

1. In *contrast* to a car, which has four wheels and an engine, a bicycle _____

_____

2. The police asked him to *identify* the man in the photograph, but _____

_____

3. In her remarks *opposing* the plan to close the old hospital, the mayor _____

_____

© Pearson Education, Inc. All rights reserved.

Name _____ Date _____

"The Highwayman" by Alfred Noyes
Take Notes for Discussion

Before the Group Discussion: Read the following passage from the poem.

And dark in the dark old innyard…before the morning light;

During the Discussion: As you discuss each question, take notes on how other students' ideas either differ from or build upon your own.

Discussion Questions	Other Ideas Expressed	Comparison to My Own Ideas
1. What does Tim plan to do with the information he overhears? Why?		
2. How do the descriptions of Tim's actions and physical appearance characterize him as a villain or a hero?		

Name _____ Date _____

"The Highwayman" by Alfred Noyes
Take Notes for Writing to Sources

Planning Your Informative Text: Before you begin drafting your **character analysis,** use the chart below to organize your ideas. Follow the directions at the top of each section.

1. Write your thesis sentence in which you state your main idea about the highwayman. You will use this as you draft your introduction and as the central idea of your analysis.

_____

_____

_____

_____

2. List the reasons that support your thesis. Under each reason, cite details from the poem that support your idea.

_____

_____

_____

_____

_____

_____

_____

_____

_____

_____

3. Jot down notes for your conclusion. Summarize your main ideas, and include an explanation of why the poet characterized the highwayman as he did.

_____

_____

_____

_____

© Pearson Education, Inc. All rights reserved.

Name _____ Date _____

"The Highwayman" by Alfred Noyes
Take Notes for Research

As you research **an outlaw hero of folk literature,** use the forms below to take notes from your sources. As necessary, continue your notes on the back of this page, on note cards, or in a word-processing document.

Source Information   Check one: ☐ Primary Source   ☐ Secondary Source

Title: _____ Author: _____

Publication Information: _____

Page(s): _____

Main Idea: _____

_____

Quotation or Paraphrase: _____

_____

Source Information   Check one: ☐ Primary Source   ☐ Secondary Source

Title: _____ Author: _____

Publication Information: _____

Page(s): _____

Main Idea: _____

_____

Quotation or Paraphrase: _____

_____

Source Information   Check one: ☐ Primary Source   ☐ Secondary Source

Title: _____ Author: _____

Publication Information: _____

Page(s): _____

Main Idea: _____

_____

Quotation or Paraphrase: _____

_____

Name _____ Date _____

"Carnegie Hero Fund Commission"
Vocabulary Builder

Selection Vocabulary

commemorated   eligible   prompted

A. DIRECTIONS: *Follow each direction. Write each response in a full sentence.*

1. Explain why a certain date might be *commemorated.* _____

   _____

2. Tell what event *prompted* Carnegie to establish the commission to recognize citizen heroes. _____

   _____

3. Who is not *eligible* to play on a sports team in your school? _____

   _____

Academic Vocabulary

characteristic   commonly   explain

B. DIRECTIONS: *Write at least one synonym and an example sentence for each word. Synonyms can be words or phrases.*

Word	Synonym	Example Sentence
explain		
commonly		
characteristic		

© Pearson Education, Inc. All rights reserved.

Name _____ Date _____

"Carnegie Hero Fund Commission"
Take Notes for Discussion

Before the Group Discussion: Read the following passage from the selection.

The Commission's definition of a hero has been largely unchanged since 1904:
A civilian who knowingly risks his or her own life to an extraordinary degree
while saving or attempting to save the life of another person.

During the Discussion: As you discuss and debate each question, take notes on how other students' ideas either differ from or build upon your own.

Discussion Questions	Other Ideas Expressed	Comparison to My Own Ideas
1. Why are professional "heroes" like policemen, firemen, and soldiers not eligible?		
2. Why do you think these restrictions are in place? Do you agree with them? Why or why not?		

Name _____ Date _____

"Carnegie Hero Fund Commission"
Take Notes for Research

As you research **the story of a past winner of the Carnegie Hero Fund Commission,** use the chart below to take notes from your sources. As necessary, continue your notes on the back of this page, on note cards, or in a word-processing document.

Winner of the Carnegie Hero Fund Commission	
Main Idea _____ _____	Main Idea _____ _____
Quotation or Paraphrase _____ _____ _____ _____ _____	Quotation or Paraphrase _____ _____ _____ _____ _____
Source Information _____ _____ _____ _____ _____	Source Information _____ _____ _____ _____ _____
Main Idea _____ _____	Main Idea _____ _____
Quotation or Paraphrase _____ _____ _____ _____ _____	Quotation or Paraphrase _____ _____ _____ _____ _____
Source Information _____ _____ _____ _____ _____	Source Information _____ _____ _____ _____ _____

© Pearson Education, Inc. All rights reserved.

Name _____ Date _____

Take Notes for Writing to Sources

Planning Your Persuasive Letter: Before you begin drafting your **persuasive letter,** use the chart below to organize your ideas. Follow the directions in each section.

---

1. Identify the person you will nominate.

_____

_____

_____

_____

---

2. Describe what the person did. List details and describe the outcome.

_____

_____

_____

_____

_____

_____

_____

_____

_____

---

3. List ways in which the person risked his or her life to save someone else.

_____

_____

_____

_____

_____

_____

_____

---

4. Jot notes for your conclusion in which you summarize your reasons why the person acted heroically and deserves the Carnegie Medal.

_____

_____

_____

_____

_____

© Pearson Education, Inc. All rights reserved.

"The Myth of the Outlaw" by Ruth M. Hamel
Vocabulary Builder

Selection Vocabulary

commissioned   nondescript   repulsive

A. DIRECTIONS: *Decide whether each statement below is true or false. On the line before each item, write TRUE or FALSE. Then explain your answers.*

_____ 1. The old cowboy was rather *nondescript* with his deeply creased face, squared-off jaw, shaggy gray hair, and a long red scar that marked his left cheek.

_____.

_____ 2. The *repulsive* meal made their mouths water, and they hurried to seat themselves around the table.

_____.

_____ 3. The councilperson was *commissioned* to serve as mayor until the election could be held.

_____.

Academic Vocabulary

attitude   reflect   viewpoint

B. DIRECTIONS: *Write the letter of the word or phrase that is the best synonym for the italicized word. Then use the italicized word in a complete sentence.*

_____ 1. *attitude*

    A. lack of an opinion   C. experience

    B. outlook   D. intelligence

_____

_____ 2. *reflect*

    A. echo   C. dismiss

    B. make up ideas   D. disguise

_____

_____ 3. *viewpoint*

    A. stubbornness   C. excitement

    B. disinterest   D. way of thinking

© Pearson Education, Inc. All rights reserved.

Name _____ Date _____

Take Notes for Discussion

Before the Group Discussion: Read the following passage from the selection.

When artist Thomas Hart Benton was commissioned to paint a mural celebrating the state of Missouri at the state capitol in 1935, he included a handsome picture of James. In addition, one of Benton's best-known lithographs is of James killing two men during a train robbery.

During the Discussion: As you discuss each question, take notes on how others' ideas either differ from or build upon your own.

Discussion Questions	Other Ideas Expressed	Comparison to My Own Ideas
1. What does James's portrayal in the state capitol mural suggest about the state's attitude toward him?		
2. Can art, such as Benton's, affect the way in which people perceive a hero or an outlaw? Explain.		

Name _____ Date _____

"The Myth of the Outlaw" by Ruth M. Hamel
Take Notes for Research

As you research **a famous outlaw of the post-Civil War era,** use the forms below to take notes from your sources. As necessary, continue your notes on the back of this page, on note cards, or in a word-processing document.

Source Information   Check one: ☐ Primary Source   ☐ Secondary Source

Title: _____   Author: _____

Publication Information: _____

Page(s): _____

Main Idea: _____

_____

Quotation or Paraphrase: _____

_____

Source Information   Check one: ☐ Primary Source   ☐ Secondary Source

Title: _____   Author: _____

Publication Information: _____

Page(s): _____

Main Idea: _____

_____

Quotation or Paraphrase: _____

_____

Source Information   Check one: ☐ Primary Source   ☐ Secondary Source

Title: _____   Author: _____

Publication Information: _____

Page(s): _____

Main Idea: _____

_____

Quotation or Paraphrase: _____

_____

© Pearson Education, Inc. All rights reserved.

Name _____ Date _____

Take Notes for Writing to Sources

Planning Your Argument: Before you begin drafting your **argument,** use the chart below to organize your ideas. Follow the directions in each section.

---

1. State your position. You will use this statement in your opening paragraph.

_____

_____

_____

_____

---

2. List your reasons for your position. Under each reason, list facts, examples, and other evidence to support your reason.

_____

_____

_____

_____

_____

_____

_____

_____

_____

---

3. List opposing arguments. Jot ideas for how you can refute these arguments.

_____

_____

_____

_____

_____

---

4. Jot down notes for your conclusion. Summarize your argument and restate your position.

_____

_____

_____

_____

_____

© Pearson Education, Inc. All rights reserved.

Name _____ Date _____

Selection Vocabulary

discipline   emphatic   gauge

A. DIRECTIONS: *Write the correct word from the list on each line.*

1. The cowboys tried to _____ the mood of the cattle by the way the animals moved and the cries they uttered.

2. Settlers had a(n) _____ message for cowboys: STAY OUT!

3. Bosses like Charles Goodnight needed to impose _____ along the trail.

Academic Vocabulary

attitude   challenge   evaluate

B. DIRECTIONS: *Complete each sentence with a word, phrase, or clause that contains a context clue for the italicized word.*

1. One of the *challenges* of a cowboy's life is _____
_____.

2. A cowboy that has a bad *attitude* toward horses _____
_____.

3. When cowboys *evaluate* a horse, they might consider _____
_____.

"The Real Story of a Cowboy's Life" by Geoffrey C. Ward
Take Notes for Discussion

Before the Debate: Read the following passage from the selection.

> The settlers' hostility was entirely understandable...and went home after we had passed.

During the Debate: As you discuss and debate each question, take notes on how other students' ideas either differ from or build upon your own.

Discussion Questions	Other Ideas Expressed	Comparison to My Own Ideas
1. Should decades of cattle drives have established the cowboys' rights to the land? Why or why not?		
2. Could a compromise have been reached? Explain.		

© Pearson Education, Inc. All rights reserved.

Name _____ Date _____

"The Real Story of a Cowboy's Life" by Geoffrey C. Ward
Take Notes for Research

As you research **settlers of the 1880s and the challenges they faced,** you can use the organizer below to take notes from your sources. As necessary, continue your notes on the back of this page, on note cards, or in a word-processing document.

Settlers of the 1880s	
Main Idea _____ _____ Quotation or Paraphrase _____ _____ _____ _____ _____ Source Information _____ _____ _____ _____	Main Idea _____ _____ Quotation or Paraphrase _____ _____ _____ _____ _____ Source Information _____ _____ _____ _____
Main Idea _____ Quotation or Paraphrase _____ _____ _____ _____ _____ Source Information _____ _____ _____ _____	Main Idea _____ Quotation or Paraphrase _____ _____ _____ _____ _____ Source Information _____ _____ _____ _____

© Pearson Education, Inc. All rights reserved.

Name _____ Date _____

"The Real Story of a Cowboy's Life" by Geoffrey C. Ward
Take Notes for Writing to Sources

Planning Your Argument: Before you begin drafting your **argument,** use the chart below to organize your ideas. Follow the directions in each section.

---

1. State your position. You will use this statement in your opening paragraph.

_____

_____

_____

_____

---

2. List reasons for your position. Under each reason, list facts, examples, and other evidence to support your reason.

_____

_____

_____

_____

_____

_____

_____

_____

_____

---

3. List opposing arguments. Jot ideas for how you can refute these arguments.

_____

_____

_____

_____

_____

---

4. Jot down notes for your conclusion. Summarize your argument and restate your position.

_____

_____

_____

_____

Name _____ Date _____

"After Twenty Years" by O. Henry
Vocabulary Builder

Selection Vocabulary

intricate   simultaneously   spectators

A. DIRECTIONS: *Write the letter of the word or phrase that means* the same or about the same as *the vocabulary word. Then use the italicized word in a complete sentence.*

_____ 1. *spectators*

   A. accusers   C. friends

   B. participants   D. audience

_____

_____ 2. *intricate*

   A. simple   C. exaggerated

   B. complex   D. not knowable

_____

_____ 3. *simultaneously*

   A. separately   C. recently

   B. all together   D. later

_____

Academic Vocabulary

communicate   contradiction   contribute

B. DIRECTIONS: *Complete each sentence with a word, phrase, or clause that contains a context clue for the italicized word.*

1. Elena tried to *communicate* with her dog by _____

_____.

2. It is a *contradiction* to say he is healthy if _____

_____.

3. The young politician asked the businessperson to *contribute* _____

_____.

All-in-One Workbook
© Pearson Education, Inc. All rights reserved.
171

Name _____ Date _____

"**After Twenty Years**" by O. Henry
Take Notes for Discussion

Before the Group Discussion: Read the following passage from the selection.

Bob,

I was at the appointed place on time. When you struck the match to light your cigar I saw it was the face of the man wanted in Chicago. Somehow I couldn't do it myself, so I went around and got a plain clothes man to do the job.

Jimmy

During the Discussion: As the group discusses each question, take notes on how other students' ideas either differ from or build upon your own.

Discussion Questions	Other Ideas Expressed	Comparison to My Own Ideas
1. Was it right for Jimmy to send someone else to arrest Bob? Explain.		
2. Should Jimmy have turned Bob in? Why or why not?		

© Pearson Education, Inc. All rights reserved.

Name _____ Date _____

"After Twenty Years" by O. Henry
Take Notes for Research

As you research **one or more police officers who have been heroes,** use the forms below to take notes from your sources. As necessary, continue your notes on the back of this page, on note cards, or in a word-processing document.

Source Information   Check one: ☐ Primary Source   ☐ Secondary Source

Title: _____   Author: _____

Publication Information: _____

Page(s): _____

Main Idea: _____

_____

Quotation or Paraphrase: _____

_____

Source Information   Check one: ☐ Primary Source   ☐ Secondary Source

Title: _____   Author: _____

Publication Information: _____

Page(s): _____

Main Idea: _____

_____

Quotation or Paraphrase: _____

_____

Source Information   Check one: ☐ Primary Source   ☐ Secondary Source

Title: _____   Author: _____

Publication Information: _____

Page(s): _____

Main Idea: _____

_____

Quotation or Paraphrase: _____

_____

© Pearson Education, Inc. All rights reserved.

Name _____ Date _____

"After Twenty Years" by O. Henry
Take Notes for Writing to Sources

Planning Your Fictional Narrative: Before you begin drafting your **fictional narrative,** use the chart below to organize your ideas. Follow the directions at the top of each section of the chart.

1. List the main plot events for your new ending. Make sure your characters' actions are consistent with the beginning of O. Henry's original story.

_____

_____

_____

_____

_____

_____

_____

_____

_____

_____

_____

_____

2. Identify your conflict and your climax.

_____

_____

_____

_____

_____

_____

3. Jot notes on how you will develop the concept of "heroes and outlaws."

_____

_____

_____

_____

_____

Name _____ Date _____

"Harriet Tubman" from *Africans in America: America's Journey Through Slavery*
Vocabulary Builder

Selection Vocabulary

conferred   feigned   subjected

A. DIRECTIONS: *Write at least one synonym, one antonym, and an example sentence for each word. Synonyms and antonyms can be words or phrases.*

Word	Synonym	Antonym	Example Sentence
subjected			
feigned			
conferred			

Academic Vocabulary

media   reactions   solve

B. DIRECTIONS: *Write a response to each question. Write your answer as a complete sentence and make sure to use the italicized word in your response.*

1. What are three kinds of popular *media*? _____

   _____.

2. Tubman's biggest problem was being a slave. How did Tubman *solve* her problem?

   _____.

3. What are some common *reactions* to listening to a comedian? _____

   _____.

© Pearson Education, Inc. All rights reserved.

Name _____ Date _____

"Harriet Tubman" from *Africans in America: America's Journey Through Slavery*
Take Notes for Discussion

Before the Group Discussion: Read the following passage from the selection.

> Tubman even carried a gun, which she used to threaten the fugitives if they became too tired or decided to turn back, telling them, "You'll be free or die."

During the Discussion: As you discuss each question, take notes on how other students' ideas either differ from or build upon your own.

Discussion Questions	Other Ideas Expressed	Comparison to My Own Ideas
1. Was Tubman right in treating the fugitives this way? Why?		
2. What does Tubman's threat tell you about how she viewed her mission?		
3. Was Tubman an outlaw, a hero, or both? Why?		

© Pearson Education, Inc. All rights reserved.

Name _____ Date _____

"Harriet Tubman" from *Africans in America: America's Journey Through Slavery*
Take Notes for Research

As you research **people who helped slaves escape to freedom on the Underground Railroad,** use the organizer below to take notes from your sources. As necessary, continue your notes on the back of this page, on note cards, or in a word-processing document.

Escape to Freedom on the Underground Railroad	
Main Idea _____ _____	Main Idea _____ _____
Quotation or Paraphrase _____ _____ _____ _____ _____	Quotation or Paraphrase _____ _____ _____ _____ _____
Source Information _____ _____ _____ _____	Source Information _____ _____ _____ _____
Main Idea _____ _____	Main Idea _____ _____
Quotation or Paraphrase _____ _____ _____ _____ _____	Quotation or Paraphrase _____ _____ _____ _____ _____
Source Information _____ _____ _____ _____	Source Information _____ _____ _____ _____

"**Harriet Tubman**" from *Africans in America: America's Journey Through Slavery*
Take Notes for Writing to Sources

Planning Your Fictional Narrative: Before you begin drafting your **fictional narrative,** use the chart below to organize your ideas. Follow the directions in each section.

1. Identify three or four topics or events you will describe in entries to your diary.

_____

_____

_____

_____

2. List important details you will include for each of your entries. Include vivid details that will make the entries seem real for readers.

_____

_____

_____

_____

_____

_____

_____

_____

_____

_____

_____

_____

_____

3. Think about how you would react to these events. Jot notes about your feelings, worries, and hopes.

_____

_____

_____

_____

_____

© Pearson Education, Inc. All rights reserved.

Media: Harriet Tubman

Vocabulary Builder and Take Notes for Writing to Sources

Academic Vocabulary

conclude   convincing   facts

DIRECTIONS: *Choose the synonym, or word closest in meaning, to the vocabulary word.*

_____ 1. *convincing*   A. offensive   B. discouraging   C. persuasive

_____ 2. *facts*   A. truths   B. opinions   C. details

_____ 3. *conclude*   A. review   B. complete   C. commence

Take Notes for Writing to Sources

Planning Your Argument: Before you begin drafting your **argument,** use the chart below to organize your ideas. Follow the directions at the top of each section.

1. List the major points in the attack on Tubman.
2. List your arguments against slavery and in support of Tubman's actions.
3. List logical reasons, facts, and moral claims that support your arguments.
4. Write notes on ideas to use in your conclusion. Include a call to action.

Unit 4: Drama
Big Question Vocabulary—1

The Big Question: Do others see us more clearly than we see ourselves?

appreciate: *v.* to understand something's importance or value; other form: *appreciation*

assumption: *n.* a decision that something is true, without definite proof; other form: *assume*

bias: *n.* the act of favoring one group of people over another; other form: *biased*

define: *v.* to describe something correctly and thoroughly; other forms: *definition, defined*

reveal: *v.* to expose something that has been hidden or secret; other forms: *revealed, revealing*

A. DIRECTIONS: *In the chart, write a synonym and an antonym for each vocabulary word. Choose your answers from the words and phrases in the box. You will not use all of them.*

theory	fairness	distort	be thankful	be happy	be ungrateful	hide
characterize	uncover	proof	pride	concentrate	prejudice	

Word	Synonym	Antonym
1. appreciate		
2. assumption		
3. bias		
4. define		
5. reveal		

B. DIRECTIONS: *Write a humorous short story about a man who receives a large parrot for a pet. At first he is unhappy because he doesn't like birds. However, the parrot is so clever that the man changes his mind. Use all five vocabulary words.*

_____

_____

_____

_____

_____

_____

_____

Unit 4: Drama
Big Question Vocabulary—2

The Big Question: Do others see us more clearly than we see ourselves?

appearance: *n.* the way a person looks to other people; other forms: *appear, appearing*

focus: *v.* to direct one's attention to one specific thing; other forms: *focusing, focused*

identify: *v.* to recognize and correctly name something; other forms: *identification, identified*

ignore: *v.* to act as if something has not been seen or heard; other forms: *ignoring, ignorant*

perspective: *n.* a special way to think about something, usually influenced by one's personality and experiences

A. DIRECTIONS: *Write the vocabulary word that best completes each group of related words.*

1. avoid, neglect, forget, _____
2. attitude, viewpoint, thoughts, _____
3. looks, image, personality, _____
4. concentrate, stare, study, _____
5. classify, define, describe, _____

B. DIRECTIONS: *On the line before each sentence, write* True *if the statement is true, or* False *if it is false. If the statement is false, rewrite the sentence so that it is true.*

_____1. A person's *appearance* is his or her innermost thoughts.

_____

_____2. If the fire alarm goes off, the best course of action is to *ignore* it.

_____

_____3. To board an airplane, you must carry a suitcase in order to *identify* yourself.

_____

_____4. Activities that require you to *focus* carefully include sleeping and daydreaming.

_____

_____5. A person's *perspective* is often based on opinions and attitudes.

_____

Unit 4: Drama
Big Question Vocabulary—3

The Big Question: Do others see us more clearly than we see ourselves?

characteristic: *n.* a special quality or feature that is typical of someone or something

image: *n.* the way a person appears to others; other forms: *images, imagination, imagine*

perception: *n.* the unique way you think about someone or something; other form: *perceive*

reaction: *n.* a response to someone or something in the form of thoughts, words, or actions; other forms: *react, reactionary*

reflect: *v.* to express or show through gestures or actions; other forms: *reflection, reflected*

Karen said this to Mario, Heidi, and Ramon: "I saw a really strange looking man on the subway. He gave me a spooky feeling. Maybe he was a magician. Anyway, he was carrying a huge bag. I peeked inside and almost fainted with shock. It was a painting—a painting of ME!"

Each of Karen's friends had a different reaction to what she said.

DIRECTIONS: *Use the word(s) shown to write what each friend said to Karen.*

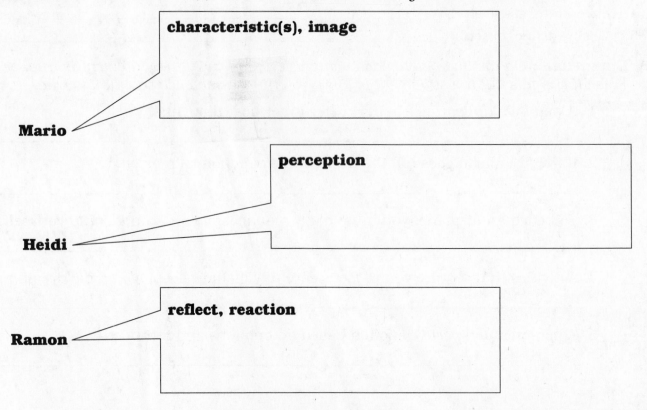

Mario

characteristic(s), image

Heidi

perception

Ramon

reflect, reaction

© Pearson Education, Inc. All rights reserved.

Name _____ Date _____

Unit 4: Drama
Applying the Big Question

Do others see us more clearly than we see ourselves?

DIRECTIONS: *Complete the chart below to apply what you have learned about how people form impressions of others. One row has been completed for you.*

Example	Who/What is Judged	Who does the Judging	Is the judgment fair?	What I learned
From Literature	Goodman in "The Monsters . . ."	His neighbors	No, it is based on the fact that he is an "oddball"	Fear can change the way people see others.
From Literature				
From Science				
From Social Studies				
From Real Life				

© Pearson Education, Inc. All rights reserved.

Name _____ Date _____

A Christmas Carol: Scrooge and Marley, *Act I* by Israel Horovitz
Writing About the Big Question

Do others see us more clearly than we see ourselves?

Big Question Vocabulary

appearance	appreciate	assumption	bias	characteristic
define	focus	identify	ignore	image
perception	perspective	reaction	reflect	reveal

A. *Choose one word from the list above to complete each sentence. There may be more than one right answer.*

1. Over time, Betsy learned to _____ her mother's fashion advice.

2. Sometimes you know what a word means, but find it hard to _____.

3. Eric's hard work in the gym helped quicken his _____ time.

B. *Follow the directions in responding to each of the items below.*

1. List two different times when you learned something new about yourself. Write your response in complete sentences.

   _____

   _____

2. Choose one of the experiences you listed in number 1. Write three or more sentences describing that experience. Use at least two of the Big Question vocabulary words. You may use the words in different forms (for example you can change *reflect* to *reflection*).

   _____

   _____

C. *Complete the sentence below. Use the completed sentence as the topic sentence in a short paragraph about the big question.*

   The way we treat others reveals _____

   _____

   _____

© Pearson Education, Inc. All rights reserved.

A Christmas Carol: Scrooge and Marley, *Act I,* by Israel Horovitz

Reading: Preview a Text to Set a Purpose for Reading

When you **set a purpose for reading,** you decide what you want to get from a text. Setting a purpose gives you a focus as you read. These are some of the reasons you might have for reading something:

- to learn about a subject
- to be entertained
- to gain understanding
- to prepare to take action or make a decision
- to find inspiration
- to complete a task

In order to set a purpose, **preview a text** before you read it. Look at the title, the pictures, the captions, the organization, and the beginnings of passages. If you already have a purpose in mind, previewing will help you decide whether the text will fit that purpose. If you do not have a purpose in mind, previewing the text will help you determine one.

DIRECTIONS: *Read the passages from Act I of* A Christmas Carol: Scrooge and Marley *indicated below, and then complete each item.*

1. Following the list of "The People of the Play," read the information labeled "The Place of the Play." Where is the play set?

   _____

2. Read the information labeled "The Time of the Play." When does the play take place?

   _____

3. What purpose or purposes might you set based on that information?

   _____

   _____

4. The illustrations that accompany the text of Act I of the play are photographs from a production of the play. Look at those photographs now, but ignore the one of the ghostly character in chains. How are the characters dressed?

   _____

5. Based on that information, what purpose might you set for reading Act I of the play?

   _____

6. Read the opening lines of Act I, Scene 1, spoken by a character called Marley. Then, look at the photograph of the ghostly character in chains. What purpose might you set based on that information?

   _____

A Christmas Carol: Scrooge and Marley, *Act I*, by Israel Horovitz
Literary Analysis: Dialogue

Dialogue is a conversation between characters. In a play, the characters are developed almost entirely through dialogue. Dialogue also advances the action of the plot and develops the conflict.

In the script of a dramatic work, you can tell which character is speaking by the name that appears before the character's lines. In this example of dialogue, you are introduced to two of the characters in *A Christmas Carol: Scrooge and Marley:*

> **NEPHEW.** [*Cheerfully; surprising* SCROOGE] A merry Christmas to you, Uncle! God save you!
>
> **SCROOGE.** Bah! Humbug!
>
> **NEPHEW.** Christmas a "humbug," Uncle? I'm sure you don't mean that.
>
> **SCROOGE.** I do! Merry Christmas? What right do you have to be merry? What reason have you to be merry? You're poor enough!

In just a few words apiece, the characters establish a conflict between them. The nephew thinks Christmas is a joyful holiday, and Scrooge thinks it is nonsense. This conflict will reappear throughout the play until it is resolved. Those lines of dialogue also give you a look at the character traits of Scrooge and his nephew. Scrooge is quarrelsome and unpleasant; the nephew is upbeat and friendly.

DIRECTIONS: *Answer the following questions about this passage from* A Christmas Carol: Scrooge and Marley, *Act I, Scene 2.*

> **PORTLY MAN.** . . . [*Pen in hand; as well as notepad*] What shall I put you down for, sir?
>
> **SCROOGE.** Nothing!
>
> **PORTLY MAN.** You wish to be left anonymous?
>
> **SCROOGE.** I wish to be left alone! [*Pauses; turns away; turns back to them*] Since you ask me what I wish, gentlemen, that is my answer. I help to support the establishments that I have mentioned; they cost enough: and those who are badly off must go there.
>
> **THIN MAN.** Many can't go there; and many would rather die.
>
> **SCROOGE.** If they would rather die, they had better do it, and decrease the surplus population. . . .

1. How many characters are speaking? Who are they?

   _____

2. What is Scrooge like in this scene?

   _____

3. How is he different from the men he is talking to?

   _____

   _____

4. Based on the identification of the characters, whom would you expect to speak next?

   _____

All-in-One Workbook
© Pearson Education, Inc. All rights reserved.
186

A Christmas Carol: Scrooge and Marley, *Act I,* by Israel Horovitz
Vocabulary Builder

Word List

conveyed   destitute   implored   morose   void

A. DIRECTIONS: *Think about the meaning of the italicized word from the Word List in each sentence. Then, answer the question, and explain your answer.*

1. Marley *implored* Scrooge to pay attention to him. Did Marley ask casually?

   _____

2. Scrooge was *morose.* Did he enjoy celebrating Christmas?

   _____

3. Are the *destitute* able to save money?

   _____

4. Scrooge looked into the *void.* Did he see anything?

   _____

5. In Act I, Scene 3, of *A Christmas Carol: Scrooge and Marley,* has Scrooge *conveyed* his fear?

   _____

   _____

B. WORD STUDY: *The Lation root -grat- means "thankful, pleasing." Read the following sentences. Use your knowledge of the root -grat- to write a full sentence to answer each question. Include the italicized word in your answer.*

1. If you are *grateful,* is it likely that someone has done something nice for you?

   _____

2. Is *gratitude* an unhappy emotion?

   _____

3. Would you value a *gratifying* friendship?

   _____

   _____

© Pearson Education, Inc. All rights reserved.

Name _____ Date _____

A Christmas Carol: Scrooge and Marley, **Act I,** by Israel Horovitz
Conventions: Prepositions and Prepositional Phrases

A **preposition** relates a noun or pronoun that follows the preposition to another word in the sentence. In *The key is in the lock,* the preposition *in* relates *lock* to *key.* These are some common prepositions:

above	below	from	of	over	under
around	by	in	on	through	up
behind	for	into	outside	to	with

A **prepositional phrase** begins with a preposition and ends with the noun or pronoun that follows it. In *The key is in the lock,* the prepositional phrase is *in the lock.*

A. DIRECTIONS: *The following sentences are from* A Christmas Carol: Scrooge and Marley. *In each sentence, circle the prepositional phrases, and underline each preposition.*

1. The spotlight is tight on Scrooge's head and shoulders.
2. He and I were partners for I don't know how many years.
3. Scrooge is busy in his counting house.
4. Cratchit . . . tries to heat his hands around his candle.
5. Next, you'll be asking to replenish your coal from my coalbox . . . .
6. You keep Christmas in your own way and let me keep it in mine.
7. There are many things from which I have derived good, by which I have not profited . . . .
8. Let me hear another sound from you and you'll keep your Christmas by losing your situation.

B. Writing Application: *Write a paragraph about a holiday you like or one you don't like. Use at least three prepositional phrases. Underline each preposition, and circle the prepositional phrases.*

_____

_____

_____

_____

_____

© Pearson Education, Inc. All rights reserved.

A Christmas Carol: Scrooge and Marley, *Act I,* by Israel Horovitz
Support for Writing to Sources: Letter

Use this form to prepare to **write a letter** to Scrooge.

Salutation

State your main point: Scrooge is missing out in life by being cranky and negative with the people around him.

State a specific thing that Scrooge is missing out on. Include a detail from the play or from your experience to support your point.

State another specific thing that Scrooge is missing out on. Include a detail from the play or from your experience to support your point.

Conclude with a summary or a request that Scrooge change his behavior.

Closing, Signature

Dear _____,

_____

_____

_____

_____

_____

_____

_____

_____

_____

_____

_____

_____

_____

_____

_____

_____

_____

_____

_____

_____

_____

_____

_____

                                        _____

                                        _____

Now, prepare a final draft of your letter.

© Pearson Education, Inc. All rights reserved.

Name _____   Date _____

A Christmas Carol: Scrooge and Marley, Act I, by Israel Horovitz
Support for Research and Technology: Costume Plans

With the members of your group, consider the garments—the articles of clothing—that you must find out about in order to prepare **costume plans** for any two characters in *A Christmas Carol: Scrooge and Marley.* You will most likely want to consider these items:

men's pants	men's vest	men's tie	women's dress
men's shirt	men's jacket	men's hat	women's hat

You might each choose two or three garments to research. Remember that you are researching the clothing that people of Scrooge's class would have worn in England in the 1840s. Enter the information on this chart.

Garment	Description of Garment, Including Type of Fabric and Color

© Pearson Education, Inc. All rights reserved.

A Christmas Carol: Scrooge and Marley, *Act II* by Israel Horovitz

Writing About the Big Question

Do others see us more clearly than we see ourselves?

Big Question Vocabulary

appearance	appreciate	assumption	bias	characteristic
define	focus	identify	ignore	image
perception	perspective	reaction	reflect	reveal

A. *Choose one word from the list above to complete each sentence. There may be more than one right answer.*

1. Do you think someone's _____ can tell you something about their personality?

2. The players felt that the coach had a _____ against short players.

3. Luke found it difficult to _____ on his work in the noisy classroom.

B. *Follow the directions in responding to each of the items below.*

1. Make a list of four or more different ways people can communicate. For example, people can communicate by *telephone*. Write your response in a complete sentence.

   _____

   _____

2. Choose one of the means of communication you listed in question 1. Write three or more sentences describing the good and bad points of communicating that way. Use at least two of the Big Question vocabulary words. You may use the words in different forms (for example you can change *reflect* to *reflection*).

   _____

   _____

C. *Complete the sentence below. Then, write a short paragraph in which you connect this sentence to the big question.*

   In order to change, we must first identify _____

   _____

   _____

© Pearson Education, Inc. All rights reserved.

Name _____ Date _____

A Christmas Carol: Scrooge and Marley, *Act II*, by Israel Horovitz
Reading: Adjust Your Reading Rate to Suit Your Purpose

Setting a purpose for reading is deciding before you read what you want to get out of a text. The purpose you set will affect the way you read.

Adjust your reading rate to suit your purpose. When you read a play, follow these guidelines:

- Read stage directions slowly and carefully. They describe action that may not be revealed by the dialogue.
- Read short lines of dialogue quickly in order to create the feeling of conversation.
- Read longer speeches by a single character slowly in order to reflect on the character's words and look for clues to the message.

DIRECTIONS: *Read the following passages, and answer the questions that follow each one.*

MAN # **1.** Hey, you, watch where you're going.

MAN # **2.** Watch it yourself, mate!

[PRESENT *sprinkles them directly, they change.*]

MAN # **1.** I pray go in ahead of me. It's Christmas. You be first!

MAN # **2.** No, no. I must insist that YOU be first!

1. How would you read the preceding dialogue? Why?

   _____

2. How would you read the stage directions? Why?

   _____

3. What important information do the stage directions contain? How does it affect your understanding of the lines that follow it?

   _____

   _____

PRESENT. Mark my words, Ebenezer Scrooge. I do not present the Cratchits to you because they are a handsome, or brilliant family. They are not handsome. They are not brilliant. They are not well-dressed, or tasteful to the times. Their shoes are not even waterproofed by virtue of money or cleverness spent. So when the pavement is wet, so are the insides of their shoes and the tops of their toes. They are the Cratchits, Mr. Scrooge. They are not highly special. They are happy, grateful, pleased with one another, contented with the time and how it passes. They don't sing very well, do they? But, nonetheless, they do sing . . . [*Pauses*] think of that, Scrooge. Fifteen shillings a week and they do sing . . . hear their song until its end.

4. How would you read the preceding passage? Why?

   _____

   _____

© Pearson Education, Inc. All rights reserved.

A Christmas Carol: Scrooge and Marley, *Act II,* by Israel Horovitz
Literary Analysis: Stage Directions

Stage directions are the words in the script of a drama that are not spoken by characters. When a play is performed, you can see the set, the characters, and the movements, and you can hear the sound effects. When you read a play, you get this information from the stage directions. Stage directions are usually printed in italic type and set off by brackets or parentheses.

DIRECTIONS: *Read the following passages, and answer the questions that follow each one.*

[BOB CRATCHIT *enters, carrying* TINY TIM *atop his shoulder. He wears a threadbare and fringe-less comforter hanging down in front of him.* TINY TIM *carries small crutches and his small legs are bound in an iron frame brace.*]

1. Who appears in this scene?

   _____

2. What does the description of Bob Cratchit reveal about the Cratchit family?

   _____

3. What does the description of Tiny Tim reveal about him?

   _____

   _____

SCROOGE. Specter, something informs me that our parting moment is at hand. I know it, but I know not how I know it.

[FUTURE *points to the other side of the stage. Lights out on* CRATCHITS. FUTURE *moves slow-ing, gliding . . .* FUTURE *points opposite.* FUTURE *leads* SCROOGE *to a wall and a tombstone. He points to the stone.*]

Am I that man those ghoulish parasites so gloated over?

4. Who appears in this scene? How do you know?

   _____

   _____

5. What do the stage directions reveal that the dialogue does not reveal?

   _____

   _____

   _____

A Christmas Carol: Scrooge and Marley, *Act II,* by Israel Horovitz
Vocabulary Builder

Word List

astonish   audible   compulsion   meager   severe

A. DIRECTIONS: *Think about the meaning of the italicized word from the Word List in each sentence. Then, answer the question, and explain your answer.*

1. Scrooge's new attitude will *astonish* his family. Will they be surprised by it?

   _____

2. Scrooge has a *compulsion* to go with each of the ghosts. Can he easily resist going?

   _____

3. Mrs. Cratchit's judgment of Scrooge is *severe*. Does she think highly of him?

   _____

4. Scrooge paid Cratchit a *meager* salary. Was the salary generous?

   _____

5. The actor's voice is *audible* when he whispers. Can the audience hear him?

   _____

B. WORD STUDY: *The Latin prefix* inter- *means "between, among." Read the following sentences. Use your knowledge of the prefix* inter- *to write a full sentence to answer each question. Include the italicized word in your answer.*

1. Have your parents ever *interceded* on your behalf?

   _____

2. If a ball is *intercepted*, does it reach its destination?

   _____

3. Is a highway *intersection* a place where two roads meet?

   _____

A Christmas Carol: Scrooge and Marley, **Act II** by Israel Horovitz

Conventions: Appositives and Appositive Phrases

An **appositive** is a noun or pronoun that is placed after another noun or pronoun to identify, rename, or explain it. In the following sentence, the appositive is underlined:

Jacob Marley, a <u>ghost</u>, was once Scrooge's partner.

An **appositive phrase** is a noun or pronoun, along with any modifiers, that is placed after another noun or pronoun to identify, rename, or explain it. In the following sentence, the appositive is underlined; the words that make up the appositive phrase are in italics:

Scrooge's nephew, *a cheerful young <u>man</u>*, invites Uncle Scrooge to his home.

A. PRACTICE: *In each sentence, underline the appositive phrase. Then, circle the noun that the appositive phrase identifies or explains.*

1. Bob Cratchit, Scrooge's clerk, works hard on Christmas Eve.

2. Later, Bob goes home to his family, a jolly bunch.

3. Scrooge, an ungenerous, grouchy person, refuses to give money to help the poor.

4. Scrooge receives a visit from The Ghost of Christmas Past, a spirit carrying a fresh holly branch.

5. The Ghost of Christmas Past, a guide to Scrooge's past, takes Scrooge on a tour of his boyhood and young manhood.

6. *A Christmas Carol,* a short novel by Charles Dickens, is the basis for this play.

B. Writing Application: *Use each phrase in brackets as an appositive phrase in the sentence that follows it. Set off each phrase with commas or dashes.*

1. [an English novelist] Charles Dickens published *A Christmas Carol* in 1843.

   _____

   _____

2. [a short novel] *A Christmas Carol* is a novella.

   _____

3. [the novella's main character] Scrooge became so famous that today his name is still a synonym for "a stingy, miserly person."

   _____

   _____

© Pearson Education, Inc. All rights reserved.

Name _____ Date _____

A Christmas Carol: Scrooge and Marley, *Act II*, by Israel Horovitz
Support for Writing to Sources: Tribute

To prepare to write a **tribute,** or an expression of admiration, to the changed Ebenezer Scrooge, answer the following questions.

What is Scrooge like before the change?

_____

_____

What anecdotes—brief stories that make a point—illustrate Scrooge's character before the change?

_____

_____

_____

_____

What causes Scrooge to change?

_____

_____

_____

What is Scrooge like after the change?

_____

_____

What anecdotes illustrate Scrooge's character after the change?

_____

_____

_____

_____

Now, write a draft of your tribute to Scrooge. Be sure to explain how Scrooge has changed and why his new behavior deserves to be honored. Use this space to write your first draft.

_____

_____

_____

_____

© Pearson Education, Inc. All rights reserved.

Name _____ Date _____

A Christmas Carol: Scrooge and Marley, Act II, by Israel Horovitz
Support for Speaking and Listening: Dramatic Monologue

You must base your **dramatic monologue** on Scrooge's thoughts as he interacts with The Ghost of Christmas Present or the Ghost of Christmas Future. As you prepare your monologue, answer these questions:

On which scene and with which ghost will you focus your monologue? (Be specific.)

_____

What is happening in this scene? _____

_____

How does Scrooge feel in this scene? Is he excited, eager, anxious, frightened?

_____

Now, write a draft of your monologue. Remember to speak as if you were Scrooge: Use the pronouns *I, me, my, mine,* and *myself.* Practice presenting the monologue, and then revise your draft to correct any weaknesses you notice.

_____

_____

_____

_____

_____

_____

_____

_____

_____

_____

_____

_____

_____

_____

_____

_____

_____

© Pearson Education, Inc. All rights reserved.

Argumentative Texts by Rachel F., San Diego, CA, and San Diego Zoo Staff
Writing About the Big Question

Do others see us more clearly than we see ourselves?

Big Question Vocabulary

appearance	appreciate	assumption	bias	characteristic
define	focus	identify	ignore	image
perception	perspective	reaction	reflect	reveal

A. *Choose one word from the list above to complete each sentence. There may be more than one right answer.*

1. Some musicians work very hard to create the right _____ for their band.

2. An older person's _____ on a problem may be different from a child's.

3. What we see, smell, taste, hear, and feel adds up to our _____ of the world.

B. *Follow the directions in responding to each of the items below.*

1. List at least two different ways people may get the wrong impression of another person. Write your response in complete sentences.

   _____

   _____

2. If you could see yourself as others do, would you want to? Write at least three sentences explaining your position. Use at least two of the Big Question vocabulary words. You may use the words in different forms (for example, you can change *reflect* to *reflection*).

   _____

   _____

C. *Complete the sentence below. Then, write a short paragraph in which you connect this sentence to the Big Question.*

The best way to understand a person is to _____

   _____

   _____

Name _____   Date _____

Reading Skill: Analyze Point of View

An editorial reflects a **writer's point of view,** or opinion, on an issue. An editorial writer uses methods such as including persuasive language or providing facts. Use the chart to help you analyze the authors' points of view in "Zoos: Joys or Jails?" and "Why Do We Need Zoos?"

DIRECTIONS: *Read the quotations. Mark an X in columns that indicate the methods the authors have used.*

Quotations (The first five quotations are from "Zoos: Joys or Jails?" The last five are from "Why Do We Need Zoos?")	**A.** Supporting statistics, facts, and examples	**B.** Persuasive techniques and language	**C.** Arguments that address opposing views	**D.** Concluding statements that reinforce authors' points of view
1. "Suddenly, you're taken from your home and shipped to a place where people come from far and wide to ogle at you...."				
2. "Sometimes, your captors force you to perform for thousands of people."				
3. "Although the idea of education to protect and preserve animals is excellent, is the zoo really setting a good example of treatment...?"				
4. "Some...say that zoos protect and save endangered species. Despite today's advanced breeding techniques, animals raised in the zoo...are not learning the survival techniques they would in the wild."				
5. "Next time you visit a zoo, look at the enclosure of the tigers and watch the seals balance a ball on their noses, and then think about what you are really learning from your day at the zoo."				
6. "The idea of a zoo actually started a long time ago, in the ancient cultures of China, the Middle East, and then the Roman Empire."				
7. "These days we also have cable TV, though, and there are lots of wild animal shows that we can watch. So why still have zoos? One of the most important reasons is conservation."				
8. "Some people feel that there is lots of wild space and that animals should only live there. Other people feel that there is very little wild space left...and it is up to us to take care of [wild animals] the best we can."				
9. "It's amazing to come almost face to face with an elephant or tiger...to feel its power, to look in its eyes; or to see an orangutan or gorilla amble right by you, holding its baby or playing chase with its brother or sister."				
10. "Zoos may be the last stand for wild species, the place where humans can grow to love them, and then work to protect them."				

Name _____ Date _____

Argumentative Texts by Rachel F., San Diego, CA, and San Diego Zoo Staff
Vocabulary Builder

Word List

    habitats   vulnerable

A. DIRECTIONS: *Complete these word maps by writing synonyms, antonyms, and an example sentence for each vocabulary word.*

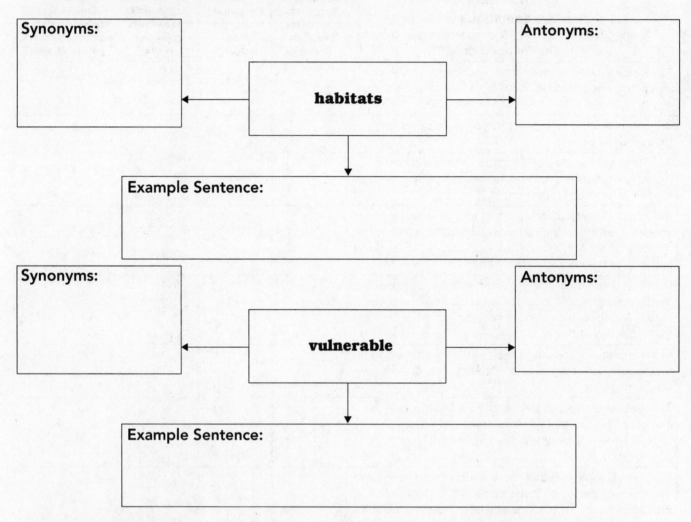

B. DIRECTIONS: *Write the letter of the word or words whose meaning is most nearly* the same as *the word from the Word List.*

___ **1.** habitats
    A. structures   **B.** burrows   **C.** territories   **D.** customs

___ **2.** vulnerable
    A. sensitized   **B.** fragile   **C.** uncertain   **D.** exquisite

© Pearson Education, Inc. All rights reserved.

Argumentative Texts by Rachel F., San Diego, CA, and San Diego Zoo Staff
Support for Writing to Sources: Editorial

Prewriting: Gathering Details

Choose an issue that affects your community or the entire United States. Use the following graphic organizer to gather reasons, facts, descriptions, and examples in support of your claims.

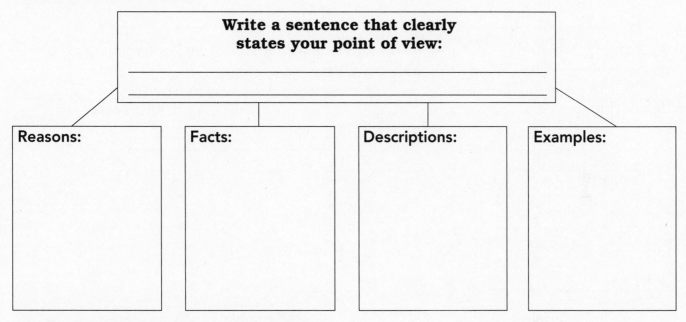

Drafting: Organizing Your Arguments

Use the following graphic organizer to list the supporting evidence you have gathered, starting with your least important points at the top and building toward your most important ones.

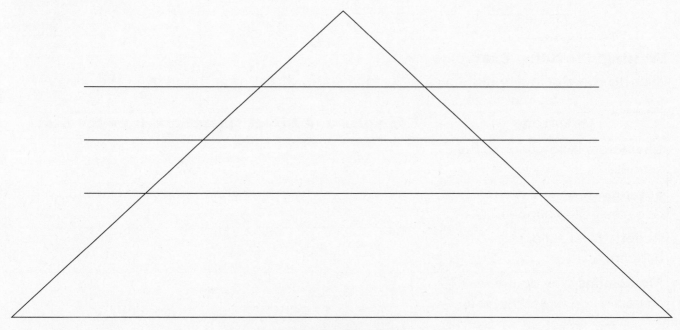

Name _____ Date _____

Writing Process
Response to Literature: Review of a Short Story

Prewriting: Gathering Details

Closely review the story to decide what you think of it. In the top rectangle, write the story's title and its author's name. Then write one sentence that sums up your main response to the story. Use the boxes below to gather details that support your response.

```
┌─────────────────────────────────────────────────────────────┐
│ Here is my main response to this story,                       │
│ " _____ "         │
│ by _____ :         │
│ _____     │
│ _____     │
└─────────────────────────────────────────────────────────────┘
```

Detail:	Detail:	Detail:

Detail:	Detail:

Drafting: Providing Examples

Use the chart below to list specific examples and direct quotations from the story.

Questions	Examples and Direct Quotations from the Story
Characters Who performs the actions?	
Settings When and where does the action happen?	
Actions What actions happen?	
Motivations Why do the main characters do what they do?	

Name _____   Date _____

Writer's Toolbox
Sentence Fluency: Revising Sentences Using Participles

A **participle** is a verb form used as an adjective to modify a noun or a pronoun—for example, *a pot of boiling water* (present participle) or *grilled steak* (past participle). A **participial phrase** is made up of a participle and its complements and modifiers. Participial phrases can add details to descriptions—for example, *a meal cooked by her aunt*.

You can use a participle to combine two short, choppy sentences:

I do not like this story. It is boring.
I do not like this boring story.

A. DIRECTIONS: *Use a present participle or a present participial phrase to combine each pair of choppy sentences. Underline the present participle in your new sentence.*

1. I love this story. It excites me. _____

2. I don't like this story. It totally confuses me. _____

_____

3. I like this character. She fascinates me. _____

4. I'm not sure how I feel about this character. In a delightful way, he irritates me.

_____

B. DIRECTIONS: *Use a past participle or a past participial phrase to combine each pair of choppy sentences from a short story. Underline the past participle in your new sentence.*

Example: My dog Hollie was in our house. The house was deserted.
My dog Hollie was in our <u>deserted</u> house.

1. The squirrel was excited by finding an acorn. The squirrel ran by the window.

_____

2. Hollie was excited by the speedy squirrel. She jumped up on the couch.

_____

3. The window was closed. She jumped against the window and broke it.

_____

4. The window was broken. Hollie jumped through the window.

_____

5. She finally gave up trying to catch the speedy squirrel. The chase had exhausted Hollie.

_____

"The Monsters Are Due on Maple Street" by Rod Serling
Vocabulary Builder

Selection Vocabulary

defiant   flustered   persistently

A. DIRECTIONS: *Read each question, and think about the meaning of the italicized word from the list. Then answer the question and explain your answer.*

1. Would you expect a *flustered* person to speak clearly?

   _____.

2. If someone *persistently* asks a question, would you assume that she is eager to know the answer?

   _____.

3. Would a *defiant* child be likely to refuse to do his chores?

   _____.

Academic Vocabulary

affect   convince   identify

B. DIRECTIONS: *Complete each sentence with a word, phrase, or clause that contains a context clue for the italicized word.*

1. As the storm roared in, it began to *affect* the people of the harbor town who _____

   _____.

2. When Ms. Gopal asked Keri to *identify* the noun in the sentence, Keri _____

   _____.

3. I tried to *convince* my mom to let me go to basketball camp by _____

   _____.

© Pearson Education, Inc. All rights reserved.

Name _____ Date _____

"The Monsters Are Due on Maple Street" by Rod Serling
Take Notes for Discussion

Before the Panel Discussion: Read the following passage from the selection.

    FIGURE ONE. With few variations. They pick the most dangerous enemy they can find…and it's themselves. And all we need do is sit back…and watch.

    FIGURE TWO. Then I take it this place…this Maple Street…is not unique.

During the Discussion: As you discuss each question, take notes on how other students' ideas either differ from or build upon your own.

Discussion Questions	Other Ideas Expressed	Comparison to My Own Ideas
1. Why are the people of Maple Street open to attack?		
2. What makes Maple Street so ordinary?		
3. How does this science fiction teleplay provide insight into why people are easy to lead?		

All-in-One Workbook
© Pearson Education, Inc. All rights reserved.
205

Name _____ Date _____

"The Monsters Are Due on Maple Street" by Rod Serling
Take Notes for Writing to Sources

Planning Your Argument: Before you begin drafting your **argumentative essay,** use the chart below to organize your ideas. Follow the directions at the top of each section.

1. State your position. You will use this statement in your opening paragraph.

_____

_____

_____

_____

2. List your reasons for your position. Under each reason, list facts, examples, and other evidence to support your reason.

_____

_____

_____

_____

_____

_____

_____

_____

3. List opposing viewpoints. Jot ideas for how you can refute these arguments.

_____

_____

_____

_____

_____

_____

4. Jot down notes for your conclusion. Summarize your argument and restate your position.

_____

_____

_____

_____

© Pearson Education, Inc. All rights reserved.

Name _____ Date _____

"The Monsters Are Due on Maple Street" by Rod Serling
Take Notes for Research

As you research **factors that can influence people to act as a mob,** use the forms below to take notes from your sources. As necessary, continue your notes on the back of this page, on note cards, or in a word-processing document.

Source Information   Check one: ☐ Primary Source   ☐ Secondary Source

Title: _____   Author: _____

Publication Information: _____

Page(s): _____

Main Idea: _____

_____

Quotation or Paraphrase: _____

_____

Source Information   Check one: ☐ Primary Source   ☐ Secondary Source

Title: _____   Author: _____

Publication Information: _____

Page(s): _____

Main Idea: _____

_____

Quotation or Paraphrase: _____

_____

Source Information   Check one: ☐ Primary Source   ☐ Secondary Source

Title: _____   Author: _____

Publication Information: _____

Page(s): _____

Main Idea: _____

_____

Quotation or Paraphrase: _____

_____

© Pearson Education, Inc. All rights reserved.

Name _____   Date _____

"All Summer in a Day" by Ray Bradbury
Vocabulary Builder

Selection Vocabulary

resilient   slackening   vital

A. DIRECTIONS: *Read each sentence. If the italicized word is used correctly, write*
Correct *on the line. If it is not used correctly, rewrite the sentence to correct it.*

1. The speed of the rocket was *slackening* as it prepared to land on Earth. _____
   _____

2. It is said that water is *vital* to life; you can live without it. _____
   _____

3. Because Margot was *resilient,* she could not get used to the conditions on Venus.
   _____
   _____

Academic Vocabulary

awareness   environment   explain

B. DIRECTIONS: *Write a complete sentence to answer each question. For each item, use a*
vocabulary word from the list in place of the underlined words with similar meanings.

1. Why would people on Earth ever want to seek out new <u>surroundings</u> on another
   planet?
   _____
   _____

2. Do you think humans have enough <u>understanding</u> of conditions in space to travel
   to another planet?
   _____
   _____

3. Who can <u>elucidate, or clarify,</u> the technology needed for travel to a distant solar
   system?
   _____
   _____

Name _____ Date _____

"All Summer in a Day" by Ray Bradbury
Take Notes for Discussion

Before the Partner Discussion: Read the following passage from the selection.

They surged about her, caught her up and bore her, protesting, and then pleading, and then crying, back into a tunnel, a room, a closet, where they slammed and locked the door. . . .

"Ready, children?" She glanced at her watch.

"Yes!" said everyone.

"Are we all here?"

"Yes!"

During the Discussion: As you discuss each question, take notes on how your partner's ideas either differ from or build upon your own.

Discussion Questions	Other Ideas Expressed	Comparison to My Own Ideas
1. Why do all the children go along with putting Margot in the closet?	_____ _____ _____ _____ _____	_____ _____ _____ _____ _____
2. Is one child more responsible than the others, or are they all equally responsible?	_____ _____ _____ _____ _____	_____ _____ _____ _____ _____
3. What lesson might Ray Bradbury have wanted to teach through this story?	_____ _____ _____ _____ _____	_____ _____ _____ _____ _____

All-in-One Workbook
© Pearson Education, Inc. All rights reserved.

Name _____ Date _____

"All Summer in a Day" by Ray Bradbury
Take Notes for Research

As you research **bullying and what is being done to develop awareness of the problem,** use the chart below to take notes from your sources. As necessary, continue your notes on the back of this page, on note cards, or in a word-processing document.

Bullying

Main Idea _____

Quotation or Paraphrase _____

_____

_____

_____

_____

Source Information _____

_____

_____

_____

Main Idea _____

Quotation or Paraphrase _____

_____

_____

_____

_____

Source Information _____

_____

_____

_____

Main Idea _____

Quotation or Paraphrase _____

_____

_____

_____

_____

Source Information _____

_____

_____

_____

Main Idea _____

Quotation or Paraphrase _____

_____

_____

_____

_____

Source Information _____

_____

_____

_____

Name _____ Date _____

"All Summer in a Day" by Ray Bradbury
Take Notes for Writing to Sources

Planning Your Informational Text: Before you begin drafting your **news report,** use the chart below to organize your ideas. Follow the directions in each section.

---

1. Answer the questions: Who? What? When? Where? Why? How? Draw your answers from details in the story.

_____

_____

_____

_____

_____

_____

---

2. Jot down an engaging lead. Add several important details to include in your opening paragraph.

_____

_____

_____

_____

_____

_____

_____

---

3. Jot down quotations you might use from the story to add interest to your report.

_____

_____

_____

_____

_____

_____

_____

"Joseph R. McCarthy" *from* Prentice Hall United States History
Vocabulary Builder

Selection Vocabulary

furor   riveted   unscrupulous

A. DIRECTIONS: *Write the letter of the word or phrase that is the best synonym for the italicized word. Then use the italicized word in a complete sentence.*

_____ 1. *unscrupulous*

    A. lacking clarity   **C.** dishonest

    B. humorous   **D.** not provable

_____

_____ 2. *furor*

    A. peaceable   **C.** crime

    B. quiet place   **D.** commotion

_____

_____ 3. *riveted*

    A. absorbed   **C.** annoyed

    B. uninterested   **D.** discouraged

Academic Vocabulary

contributes   evaluations   tactic

B. DIRECTIONS: *Decide whether each statement below is true or false. On the line before each item, write TRUE or FALSE. Then explain your answers.*

_____ 1. I always read *evaluations* for any new product before I buy it.

_____.

_____ 2. The political committee had well-planned *tactics* so the campaign seemed completely disorganized.

_____.

_____ 3. Ms. Cohen considers it a good cause and *contributes* heavily by working for the organization and giving money to support it.

_____

© Pearson Education, Inc. All rights reserved.

Name _____ Date _____

"Joseph R. McCarthy" *from* Prentice Hall United States History
Take Notes for Discussion

Before the Debate: Read the following passage from the selection.

The American people watched as McCarthy intimidated witnesses and offered evasive responses when questioned. When he attacked a young Army lawyer, the Army's chief counsel thundered, "Have you no sense of decency, sir?" The Army-McCarthy hearings struck many observers as a shameful moment in American politics.

During the Debate: As you discuss and debate each question, take notes on how other students' ideas either differ from or build upon your own.

Discussion Questions	Other Ideas Expressed	Comparison to My Own Ideas
1. Is it ever right to pursue accusations based on a strong belief but no concrete proof? Explain.		
2. Should cameras be allowed in Senate hearings and other court proceedings? Explain.		

Name _____ Date _____

As you research **the United States Senate investigation of communism during the 1950s,** use the forms below to take notes from your sources. As necessary, continue your notes on the back of this page, on note cards, or in a word-processing document.

Source Information   Check one: ☐ Primary Source   ☐ Secondary Source

Title: _____   Author: _____

Publication Information: _____

Page(s): _____

Main Idea: _____

_____

Quotation or Paraphrase: _____

_____

Source Information   Check one: ☐ Primary Source   ☐ Secondary Source

Title: _____   Author: _____

Publication Information: _____

Page(s): _____

Main Idea: _____

_____

Quotation or Paraphrase: _____

_____

Source Information   Check one: ☐ Primary Source   ☐ Secondary Source

Title: _____   Author: _____

Publication Information: _____

Page(s): _____

Main Idea: _____

_____

Quotation or Paraphrase: _____

_____

Name _____ Date _____

Take Notes for Writing to Sources

Planning Your Argument: Before you begin drafting your **argument,** use the chart below to organize your ideas. Follow the directions in each section.

---

1. State your position. You will use this statement in your opening paragraph.

_____

_____

_____

---

2. List your reasons for your position. Under each reason, list facts, examples, and other evidence to support your reason.

_____

_____

_____

_____

_____

_____

_____

_____

_____

---

3. List opposing arguments. Jot ideas for how you can refute these arguments.

_____

_____

_____

_____

---

4. Write notes for your conclusion in which you summarize your argument and restate your position.

_____

_____

_____

_____

© Pearson Education, Inc. All rights reserved.

Name _____ Date _____

"The Salem Witch Trials of 1692"
Vocabulary Builder

Selection Vocabulary

   accusations   disbanded   successive

A. DIRECTIONS: *Write an explanation for your answer to each question.*

1. Do you think most people like to face *accusations*?

   _____.

2. If the band will play on *successive* weekends beginning this Saturday, will they perform the following weekend?

   _____.

3. If a committee is *disbanded*, will they likely meet again next week?

   _____.

Academic Vocabulary

   examine   formal   simultaneously

B. DIRECTIONS: *Complete each sentence with a word, phrase, or clause that contains a context clue for the italicized word.*

1. Henry chose to *examine* the history of witchcraft in America, so he _____

   _____.

2. Because she was supposed to write a *formal* essay, Jordana _____

   _____.

3. If the chorus hit the first note *simultaneously*, _____

   _____.

© Pearson Education, Inc. All rights reserved.

Name _____ Date _____

"The Salem Witch Trials of 1692"
Take Notes for Discussion

Before the Group Discussion: Read the following passage from the selection.

> As years passed, apologies were offered, and restitution was made to the victims' families. Historians and sociologists have examined this most complex episode in our history so that we may understand the issues of that time and apply our understanding to our own society.

During the Discussion: As you discuss each question, take notes on how other students' ideas either differ from or build upon your own.

Discussion Questions	Other Ideas Expressed	Comparison to My Own Ideas
1. Why is it important to study events that took place more than three hundred years ago?		
2. What can we learn from the Salem Witch Trials?		

© Pearson Education, Inc. All rights reserved.

Name _____ Date _____

"The Salem Witch Trials of 1692"
Take Notes for Research

As you research **mass hysteria and how it relates to the Salem Witch Trials,** you can use the organizer below to take notes from your sources. As necessary, continue your notes on the back of this page, on note cards, or in a word-processing document.

Mass Hysteria and the Salem Witch Trials	
Main Idea _____ _____	Main Idea _____ _____
Quotation or Paraphrase _____ _____ _____ _____ _____	Quotation or Paraphrase _____ _____ _____ _____ _____
Source Information _____ _____ _____ _____	Source Information _____ _____ _____ _____
Main Idea _____ _____	Main Idea _____ _____
Quotation or Paraphrase _____ _____ _____ _____ _____	Quotation or Paraphrase _____ _____ _____ _____ _____
Source Information _____ _____ _____ _____	Source Information _____ _____ _____ _____

"The Salem Witch Trials of 1692"
Take Notes for Writing to Sources

Planning Your Informational Text: Before you begin drafting your **expository essay,** use the chart below to organize your ideas. Follow the directions in each section.

1. Write notes for your introduction on the events in Salem and how they relate to mass hysteria.

_____

_____

_____

_____

2. Develop your topic. Write definitions of key terms and list details and examples you'll include in the body of the essay.

_____

_____

_____

_____

_____

_____

_____

_____

_____

_____

_____

_____

_____

_____

3. Write notes for your conclusion. Summarize your main idea.

_____

_____

_____

_____

_____

Name _____ Date _____

"Herd Mentality? The Freakonomics of Boarding a Bus" by Stephen J. Dubner
Vocabulary Builder

Selection Vocabulary

investment   muster   succumb

A. DIRECTIONS: *Write the letter of the word or phrase that means the same or about the same as the vocabulary word. Then use the italicized word in a complete sentence.*

_____ 1. *investment*

    A. interest   **C.** money

    B. banking   **D.** expenditure

_____

_____ 2. *muster*

    A. give away   **C.** energy

    B. gather   **D.** preserve

_____

_____ 3. *succumb*

    A. resist   **C.** give in

    B. lose   **D.** get out of

_____

Academic Vocabulary

assumptions   behavior   contribute

B. DIRECTIONS: *Complete each sentence with a word, phrase, or clause that contains a context clue for the italicized word.*

1. My dog's *behavior* is great until she sees another dog, and then _____

_____.

2. Each family was asked to *contribute* to the annual community street fair either by

_____

_____.

3. Sam thought his new neighbor was unfriendly, but his *assumption* was wrong because _____

_____.

Name _____ Date _____

"Herd Mentality? The Freakonomics of Boarding a Bus" by Stephen J. Dubner
Take Notes for Discussion

Before the Partner Discussion: Read the following passage from the selection.

There is a herd at Point A; people may not *like* being part of a herd, but psychologically they are somehow comforted by it; they succumb to "herd mentality" and unthinkingly tag along—because if everyone else is doing it, it must be the thing to do.

During the Discussion: As your partner discusses each question, take notes on how his or her ideas either differ from or build upon your own.

Discussion Questions	Other Ideas Expressed	Comparison to My Own Ideas
1. Why do people go along with the crowd?		
2. What evidence in the blog post shows that not everyone will follow a crowd?		

Name _____ Date _____

"Herd Mentality? The Freakonomics of Boarding a Bus" by Stephen J. Dubner
Take Notes for Research

As you research **herd mentality,** use the forms below to take notes from your sources. As necessary, continue your notes on the back of this page, on note cards, or in a word-processing document.

Source Information   Check one: ☐ Primary Source   ☐ Secondary Source

Title: _____   Author: _____

Publication Information: _____

Page(s): _____

Main Idea: _____

_____

Quotation or Paraphrase: _____

_____

Source Information   Check one: ☐ Primary Source   ☐ Secondary Source

Title: _____   Author: _____

Publication Information: _____

Page(s): _____

Main Idea: _____

_____

Quotation or Paraphrase: _____

_____

Source Information   Check one: ☐ Primary Source   ☐ Secondary Source

Title: _____   Author: _____

Publication Information: _____

Page(s): _____

Main Idea: _____

_____

Quotation or Paraphrase: _____

_____

© Pearson Education, Inc. All rights reserved.

"Herd Mentality? The Freakonomics of Boarding a Bus" by Stephen J. Dubner
Take Notes for Writing to Sources

Planning Your Autobiographical Narrative: Before you begin drafting your **autobiographical narrative,** use the chart below to organize your ideas. Follow the directions at the top of each section of the chart.

1. Identify the situation and setting and describe the main people involved in events.

_____

_____

_____

_____

_____

_____

_____

_____

2. List ways in which your experience compares to Dubner's.

_____

_____

_____

_____

3. Jot notes on how you can include description, sequence, and dialogue in your narrative.

_____

_____

_____

4. Write notes you can use in your conclusion. Consider how you can make it memorable and satisfying.

_____

_____

_____

_____

© Pearson Education, Inc. All rights reserved.

"Follow the Leader: Democracy in Herd Mentality" by Michael Schirber
Vocabulary Builder

Selection Vocabulary

explicit   inherent   pertinent

A. DIRECTIONS: *Write at least one synonym, one antonym, and an example sentence for each word. Synonyms and antonyms can be words or phrases.*

Word	Synonym	Antonym	Example Sentence
pertinent			
explicit			
inherent			

Academic Vocabulary

complex   refute   transmitting

B. DIRECTIONS: *Write a response to each question. Write your answer as a complete sentence, and make sure to use the italicized word in your response.*

1. What happens when a cell phone tower stops *transmitting* signals? _____

_____.

2. What can be done if a computer problem is too *complex* for you to solve?

_____

_____.

3. How might a lawyer try to *refute* a witness's testimony? _____

_____.

© Pearson Education, Inc. All rights reserved.

Name _____ Date _____

"Follow the Leader: Democracy in Herd Mentality" by Michael Schirber
Take Notes for Discussion

Before the Group Discussion: Read the following passage from the selection.

"In the real world, you do have individuals with different information, needs and preferences," Couzin explained. "What we show is that—using very simple rules—the group will choose the majority. It's almost like a democratic decision."

During the Discussion: As you discuss each question, take notes on how other students' ideas either differ from or build upon your own.

Discussion Questions	Other Ideas Expressed	Comparison to My Own Ideas
1. Are leaders always in the majority? Explain, using examples to support your answer.		
2. For humans, is it usually a good decision to follow the majority? Explain.		

© Pearson Education, Inc. All rights reserved.

"Follow the Leader: Democracy in Herd Mentality" by Michael Schirber
Take Notes for Research

As you research **"the wisdom of crowds,"** use the organizer below to take notes from your sources. As necessary, continue your notes on the back of this page, on note cards, or in a word-processing document.

"The Wisdom of Crowds"

Main Idea _____ _____	Main Idea _____ _____
Quotation or Paraphrase _____ _____ _____ _____ _____	Quotation or Paraphrase _____ _____ _____ _____ _____
Source Information _____ _____ _____ _____	Source Information _____ _____ _____ _____
Main Idea _____ _____	Main Idea _____ _____
Quotation or Paraphrase _____ _____ _____ _____ _____	Quotation or Paraphrase _____ _____ _____ _____ _____
Source Information _____ _____ _____ _____	Source Information _____ _____ _____ _____

© Pearson Education, Inc. All rights reserved.

"Follow the Leader: Democracy in Herd Mentality" by Michael Schirber
Take Notes for Writing to Sources

Planning Your Argument: Before you begin drafting your **argument,** use the chart below to organize your ideas. Follow the directions in each section.

1. State your claim about democratic decisions versus expert decisions. You will use this to draft your introduction.

_____

_____

_____

2. List your points of evidence: strong reasoning and evidence from your research and from the text.

_____

_____

_____

_____

_____

_____

_____

3. List counterarguments and list evidence and reasoning that refute them.

_____

_____

_____

_____

_____

4. Jot notes for your conclusion. Summarize your argument and restate your position.

_____

_____

_____

_____

© Pearson Education, Inc. All rights reserved.

Media: Martin Luther King Memorial
Vocabulary Builder and Take Notes for Research

Academic Vocabulary

image   significance   understand

DIRECTIONS: *Choose the* **synonym,** *or word closest in meaning, to the vocabulary word.*

_____ 1. *image*   A. representation   B. fiction   C. object

_____ 2. *understand*   A. question   B. believe   C. know

_____ 3. *significance*   A. estimation   B. meaning   C. deception

Take Notes for Research

As you research **the memorial and its creator, Lei Yixin,** use the forms below to take notes from your sources. As necessary, continue your notes on the back of this page, on note cards, or in a word-processing document.

Source Information   Check one: ☐ Primary Source   ☐ Secondary Source

Title: _____   Author: _____

Publication Information: _____

Page(s): _____

Main Idea: _____

_____

Quotation or Paraphrase: _____

_____

Source Information   Check one: ☐ Primary Source   ☐ Secondary Source

Title: _____   Author: _____

Publication Information: _____

Page(s): _____

Main Idea: _____

_____

Quotation or Paraphrase: _____

_____

© Pearson Education, Inc. All rights reserved.

Name _____ Date _____

Unit 5: Themes in the Oral Tradition
Big Question Vocabulary—1

The Big Question: Community or individual: Which is more important?

common: *adj.* shared with others, such as mutual ideas or interests

community: *n.* a town or neighborhood in which a group of people live; other forms: *communal, communities*

culture: *n.* the ideas, beliefs, and customs that are shared by people in a society; other forms: *cultural, cultured*

individual: *n.* a person; other form: *individually*

unique: *adj.* single, one of a kind

A. DIRECTIONS: *Follow each direction.*

1. Explain the difference between something that is **common** and something that is **unique.** Provide an example of each. _____

   _____

2. Explain the relationship between an **individual** and his or her **community.** _____

   _____

3. Provide three examples of **culture**—ideas, beliefs, or customs shared by people living in your community or in the United States at large.

   _____

   _____

   _____

B. DIRECTIONS: *Provide an example of each of the following.*

1. a common interest shared by you and a friend: _____

   _____

2. a community in which you would like to live someday: _____

   _____

3. a foreign culture of your family, neighbors, or friends: _____

   _____

4. an individual whom you admire: _____

   _____

5. a characteristic or feature that makes you unique: _____

   _____

Unit 5: Themes in the Oral Tradition
Big Question Vocabulary—2

The Big Question: Community or individual: Which is more important?

custom: *n.* a tradition shared by people from the same culture; other form: *customary.*

diversity: *n.* a variety of different ideas, cultures, or objects; other form: *diverse*

environment: *n.* the setting in which an individual lives; other form: *environmental*

group: *n.* several people or things that are together; other forms: *grouping, grouped*

duty: *n.* conduct due to parents and superiors; tasks, conduct, service, or functions that arise from one's position; other form: *dutiful*

DIRECTIONS: *Answer each question.*

1. Many snakes and colorful birds reside in a rain forest. Which vocabulary word **best** describes where they live? Explain your answer. _____
   _____

2. Sally takes care of her sisters every day when she comes home from school. Which vocabulary word **best** describes this situation? Explain your answer. _____
   _____

3. Every May 1, my sister and I make May baskets. Then we deliver them to our neighbors. Which vocabulary word **best** describes this annual event? Explain your answer.
   _____

4. Everyone interested in running the marathon got together to share their ideas about training. Which vocabulary word **best** describes these individuals? Explain your answer.
   _____

5. The restaurant serves Italian, Spanish, English, African, and German foods. Which vocabulary word **best** describes the menu? Explain your answer. _____
   _____

Unit 5: Themes in the Oral Tradition
Big Question Vocabulary—3

The Big Question: Community or individual: Which is more important?

ethnicity: *n.* the race or national group to which an individual belongs; other form: *ethnic*

family: *n.* a group of people who are related to each other; other forms: *families, familiar*

team: *n.* a group of people who work together to achieve a common goal

tradition: *n.* a belief or custom that has existed for a long time; other form: *traditional*

unify: *v.* to combine two or more things to form a single unit; other form: *unified*

DIRECTIONS: *Answer each question.*

1. Which vocabulary word is an **antonym** for the word *separate*? Explain their opposite meanings.

   _____

2. Chico and Manny's family came to this country from Spain. Which vocabulary word **best** describes their family's roots? Explain your answer. _____
   _____

3. The students in my class broke into small groups to create radio plays. Which vocabulary word **best** describes each group? Explain your answer. _____
   _____

4. On Valentine's Day each year, my mother and her friend Mrs. Ortiz make delicious heart-shaped cookies. Which vocabulary word **best** describes this annual event? Explain your answer. _____
   _____

5. I have four brothers and fifteen cousins. Which vocabulary word **best** describes this group? Explain your answer. _____
   _____

All-in-One Workbook
© Pearson Education, Inc. All rights reserved.
231

Unit 5: Themes in the Oral Tradition
Applying the Big Question

Community or individual—which is more important?

DIRECTIONS: *Complete the chart below to apply what you have learned about the importance of the community and the individual. One row has been completed for you.*

Example	What does the individual want?	What does the community want?	Who won or lost	What I learned
From Literature	Ixtla wants to marry Popo	Ixtla to rule the kingdom	Nobody, because Ixtla dies of a broken heart	Sometimes individuals cannot be forced to do what others wish of them
From Literature				
From Science				
From Social Studies				
From Real Life				

© Pearson Education, Inc. All rights reserved.

"Demeter and Persephone" by Anne Terry White
Writing About the Big Question

Community or individual: Which is more important?

Big Question Vocabulary

common	community	culture	custom	diversity
duty	environment	ethnicity	family	group
individual	team	tradition	unify	unique

A. *Use one or more words from the list above to complete each sentence.*

1. Zach and his dad had a _____ of washing their cars on Sunday.

2. However, their local _____ was experiencing a water shortage.

3. They had a _____ to consider the impact of their actions on others.

4. They decided to forgo the carwash for the _____ good of the town.

B. *Follow the directions in responding to each of the items below.*

1. Describe a time when you or someone you know was faced with a decision that would affect a large number of people. _____
   _____

2. Write two sentences explaining the decision and how it affected those involved. Use at least two of the Big Question vocabulary words.
   _____
   _____

C. *Complete the sentence below. Then, write a short paragraph in which you connect this situation to the big question.*

When making a decision that will affect the greater community, it is one's duty to

_____

_____

_____

_____

_____

_____

Name _____ Date _____

"Demeter and Persephone" by Anne Terry White

Reading: Ask Questions to Analyze Cause-and-Effect Relationships

A **cause** is an event, an action, or a feeling that produces an **effect,** or result. In some literary works, multiple causes result in one single effect. In other works, a single cause results in multiple effects. Effects can also become causes for events that follow. The linking of causes and effects propels the action forward.

As you read, **ask questions** such as "What happened?" and "What will happen as a result of this?" **to analyze cause-and-effect relationships.**

DIRECTIONS: *Use the following graphic organizer to analyze some of the cause-and-effect relationships in "Demeter and Persephone." The first response has been filled in as an example. Where there is no box in which to write the question you would ask yourself, ask the question mentally, and then write the effect in the next box.*

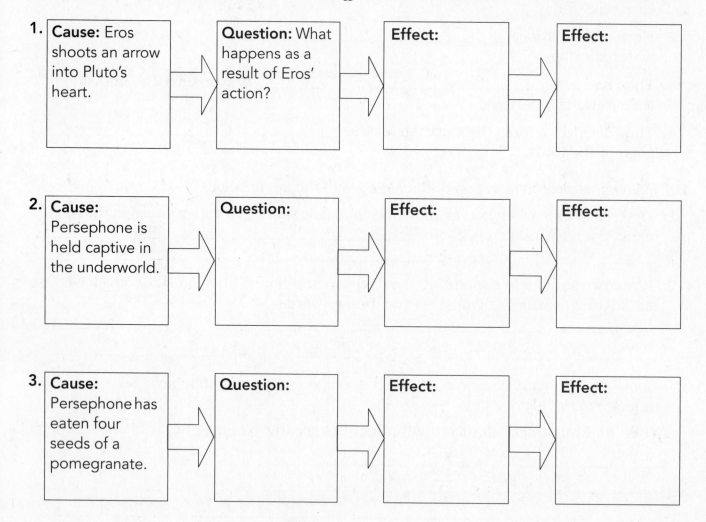

1. **Cause:** Eros shoots an arrow into Pluto's heart.

   Question: What happens as a result of Eros' action?

   Effect:

   Effect:

2. **Cause:** Persephone is held captive in the underworld.

   Question:

   Effect:

   Effect:

3. **Cause:** Persephone has eaten four seeds of a pomegranate.

   Question:

   Effect:

   Effect:

Name _____ Date _____

"Demeter and Persephone" by Anne Terry White
Literary Analysis: Myth

Since time began, people have tried to understand the world around them. Ancient peoples created **myths**—stories that explain natural occurrences and express beliefs about right and wrong. Every culture has its own collection of myths, or *mythology.* In many myths, gods and goddesses have human traits, and human heroes have superhuman traits. Myths explore universal themes and explain the world in human terms.

Most myths perform some of the following functions:

- explain natural occurrences
- express beliefs about right and wrong
- show gods or goddesses with human traits
- show human heroes with superhuman traits
- explore universal themes

Not all myths perform all of those functions, however. "Demeter and Persephone" illustrates only a few of them.

DIRECTIONS: *Read each excerpt from "Demeter and Persephone" that follows, and answer the question about the function of a myth that the excerpt illustrates.*

Deep under Mt. Aetna, the gods had buried alive a number of fearful, fire-breathing giants. The monsters heaved and struggled to get free. And so mightily did they shake the earth . . .

1. Which function of a myth does the excerpt illustrate? How can you tell?

_____

_____

_____

Now an unaccustomed warmth stole through his veins. His stern eyes softened. . . . The god looked at Persephone and loved her at once.

2. Which function of a myth does the excerpt illustrate? How can you tell?

_____

_____

_____

It seemed that all mankind would die of hunger.
"This cannot go on," said mighty Zeus. "I see that I must intervene."

3. Which function of a myth does the excerpt illustrate? How can you tell?

_____

_____

_____

© Pearson Education, Inc. All rights reserved.

Name _____ Date _____

"Demeter and Persephone" by Anne Terry White
Vocabulary Builder

Word List

abode   defies   intervene   monarch   realm

A. DIRECTIONS: *Revise each sentence so that it makes sense.*

1. Zeus is pleased when a god or goddess <u>defies</u> his orders.

   _____

2. When the world is calm and at peace, Zeus is likely to <u>intervene</u>.

   _____

3. The <u>monarch</u> bowed before his subjects.

   _____

4. Within the <u>realm</u> of fantasy, imagination is restrained.

   _____

5. With its cheerful fire and sweet scent, the Queen's <u>abode</u> gave her a sense of danger.

   _____

B. WORD STUDY: *The Latin root -dom- means "master" or "building." Answer each of the following questions using one of these words containing -dom-: domicile, dominant, domesticate.*

1. What do people do in a *domicile*?

   _____

2. If you are a *dominant* figure in politics, what kind of position would you hold?

   _____

3. What happens when you *domesticate* an animal?

   _____

© Pearson Education, Inc. All rights reserved.

Name _____ Date _____

Conventions: Infinitive Phrases and Gerund Phrases

An **infinitive** is a verb form that acts as a noun, an adjective, or an adverb. Most infinitives begin with *to*. An **infinitive phrase** is an infinitive plus its own modifiers or complements. In the examples below, the infinitive phrases are italicized and the infinitives are underlined.

Infinitive Phrases	
Noun (functioning as subject)	*To shoot an arrow straight to its target* is pretty difficult.
Adjective (modifying *guy*)	Eros is the guy *to have around* when you need an archer.
Adverb (modifying *Eager*)	Eager *to make Pluto fall in love*, Aphrodite summons Eros.

A **gerund** is a verb form that acts as a noun. It can function as a subject, an object, a predicate noun, or the object of a preposition. A **gerund phrase** is a gerund plus its own modifiers or complements. In the examples below, the phrases are italicized and the gerunds are underlined.

Gerund Phrases	
Subject	*Locating her daughter* is not easy for Demeter.
Direct Object	She makes *searching for Persephone* her mission.
Predicate Noun	Persephone enjoys *between-meal snacking*.
Object of the Preposition	She never gets tired of *eating pomegranate seeds*.

A. PRACTICE: *Underline the infinitive and infinitive phrase or the gerund and gerund phrase in each sentence. Write* infinitive *or* gerund *to identify the phrase.*

1. To lose her daughter is a terrible tragedy for Demeter. _____

2. Having Persephone with her again fills the mother with joy. _____

3. Demeter wants to keep Persephone with her all year round. _____

4. The goddess spends every winter missing her dear daughter. _____

B. Writing Application: *Answer each question with a complete sentence. Use the infinitive or gerund phrase in parentheses.*

1. What do many little kids like to do on snowy days? (sledding down hills)

_____

2. What do many people like to drink on cold winter days? (to drink hot chocolate)

_____

3. How can you tell that spring is coming? (building their nests)

_____

4. In springtime, what is a good use for a vacant lot? (to plant flowers and vegetables)

_____

© Pearson Education, Inc. All rights reserved.

Name _____ Date _____

Support for Writing to Sources: Myth

Use the following graphic organizer to take notes for a **myth** you will write to explain a natural phenomenon. You do not have to respond to each prompt in the chart in the order in which it appears, but you should probably decide on the phenomenon you want to explain before you decide on anything else. You might describe the problem and the resolution next and then work on the characters. Coming up with the title may be the last thing you do.

Natural phenomenon that myth will explain:
Title of myth:
Names and traits of characters—how they look, what they do, what they say to one another:
Problem to be solved and creative way in which it will be solved:

Now, write the first draft of your myth.

© Pearson Education, Inc. All rights reserved.

"Demeter and Persephone" by Anne Terry White
Support for Speaking and Listening: Debate

Before you present your **debate,** discuss the following points with the members of your group. Then, respond to the prompts that follow.

- Demeter was justified in changing the weather on Earth.
- Demeter was not justified in changing the weather on Earth.

My group's argument: _____

_____

Points in support of our argument: _____

_____

_____

_____

_____

_____

Expected arguments by opposition: _____

_____

_____

_____

_____

_____

Our counterarguments: _____

_____

_____

_____

_____

_____

© Pearson Education, Inc. All rights reserved.

"Popocatepetl and Ixtlaccihuatl" by Juliet Piggott Wood
Writing About the Big Question

Community or individual: Which is more important?

Big Question Vocabulary

common	community	culture	custom	diversity
duty	environment	ethnicity	family	group
individual	team	tradition	unify	unique

A. *Use one or more words from the list above to complete each sentence.*

1. Cassie's coach begins each new season with a special _____.

2. She always hosts a _____ dinner the night before the first game.

3. Cassie doesn't want to go this year, but she feels it is her _____.

4. The coach sees the dinner as a way to _____ the team.

B. *Follow the directions in responding to each of the items below.*

1. List two examples that show the value of tradition or community involvement.

_____

_____

2. Write two sentences describing one of the preceding examples and explain how it benefits those involved. Use at least two of the Big Question vocabulary words.

_____

_____

_____

_____

C. *Complete the sentences below. Then, write a short paragraph in which you connect this idea to the big question.*

Tradition and **duty** to one's **community** should _____

_____

_____

_____

_____

© Pearson Education, Inc. All rights reserved.

"Popocatepetl and Ixtlaccihuatl" by Juliet Piggott Wood

Reading: Reread to Look for Connections That Indicate Cause-and-Effect Relationships

A **cause** is an event or a situation that produces an **effect,** or the result produced. In a story or an essay, each effect may eventually become a cause for the next event. This series of events results in a cause-and-effect chain, which propels the action forward.

As you read, think about the causes and effects of events. If you do not see a clear cause-and-effect relationship in a passage, **reread to look for connections** in the text. Look for words and phrases that identify cause-and-effect relationships—for example, *because, due to, for that reason, therefore,* and *as a result.*

DIRECTIONS: *Read the following sequences of events. Underline any words or phrases that help you identify a cause-and-effect relationship. Then, identify each event as a* cause, *an* effect, *or both* cause and effect.

_____ 1. The Emperor wants Ixtla to rule the empire after he dies.

_____ 2. Therefore, Ixtla becomes more serious and more studious.

_____ 3. Ixtla also studies harder because she has fallen in love.

_____ 4. The Emperor becomes ill.

_____ 5. As a result, he rules the empire less effectively.

_____ 6. Because the empire has grown weaker, enemies are emboldened to surround it.

_____ 7. Because enemies surround the empire, the Emperor commands his warriors to defeat them.

_____ 8. Jealous warriors tell the Emperor that Popo has been killed in battle.

_____ 9. The Emperor tells Ixtla that Popo has died.

_____ 10. Because she is heartbroken and does not want to marry anyone but Popo, Ixtla grows sick and dies.

_____ 11. When Popo learns the circumstances of Ixtla's death, he kills the warriors who lied to the Emperor.

_____ 12. Popo grieves for Ixtla.

_____ 13. Therefore, Popo instructs the warriors to build two pyramids.

_____ 14. Popo stands atop the second pyramid, holding a burning torch.

_____ 15. Over time, the pyramids became mountains.

© Pearson Education, Inc. All rights reserved.

"Popocatepetl and Ixtlaccihuatl" by Juliet Piggott Wood
Literary Analysis: Legends and Facts

A **legend** is a traditional story about the past. A legend generally starts out as a story based on **fact**—something that can be proved true. Over the course of many generations, however, the story is retold and transformed into fiction. It becomes a legend.

Every culture has its own legends to immortalize real people who were famous in their time. Most legends include these elements:

- a larger-than-life hero or heroine
- fantastic events
- roots, or a basis, in historical facts
- actions and events that reflect the culture that created the legend

A powerful Aztec emperor wants to pass his kingdom on to his daughter, Ixtlaccihuatl, or Ixtla. Ixtla studies hard so that she will be worthy of this role. She loves Popocatepetl, or Popo, a brave and strong warrior in the service of the emperor. The emperor, Ixtla, and Popo are three larger-than-life characters who will form the basis of the legend.

DIRECTIONS: *Read each excerpt from "Popocatepetl and Ixtlaccihuatl." On the line, identify the element or elements of a legend that the passage reflects, and briefly explain how you recognized the element.*

1. The pass through which the Spaniards came to the ancient Tenochtitlan is still there, as are the volcanoes on each side of that pass. Their names have not been changed. The one to the north is Ixtlaccihuatl and the one on the south of the pass is Popocatepetl.

   Element of legend: _____

   Explanation: _____

2. There was once an Aztec Emperor in Tenochtitlan. He was very powerful. Some thought he was wise as well, whilst others doubted his wisdom.

   Element of legend: _____

   Explanation: _____

3. As time went on natural leaders emerged and, of these, undoubtedly Popo was the best. Finally it was he, brandishing his club and shield, who led the great charge of running warriors across the valley, with their enemies fleeing before them.

   Element of legend: _____

   Explanation: _____

4. So Popocatepetl stood there, holding the torch in memory of Ixtlaccihuatl, for the rest of his days.
   The snows came and, as the years went by, the pyramids of stone became high white-capped mountains.

   Element of legend: _____

   Explanation: _____

All-in-One Workbook
© Pearson Education, Inc. All rights reserved.
242

"Popocatepetl and Ixtlaccihuatl" by Juliet Piggott Wood
Vocabulary Builder

Word List

decreed   feebleness   relish   routed   shortsightedness

A. DIRECTIONS: *Answer each question after thinking about the meaning of the underlined word from the Word List. Then, explain your answer.*

1. When the Emperor <u>decreed</u> that the triumphant warrior would marry his daughter, did he ask a question?

   _____

2. Would the Emperor have shown <u>shortsightedness</u> by considering the needs of his kingdom after his death?

   _____

3. When the warriors <u>routed</u> the enemy, did the battles continue?

   _____

4. Did the Emperor's <u>feebleness</u> inspire him to lead his warriors into battle?

   _____

5. Did Ixtla <u>relish</u> the idea of marrying Popo?

   _____

B. WORD STUDY: *The Latin prefix* uni- *means "having or consisting of only one." Answer each of the following questions using one of these words containing* uni-: *unicycle, unicorn, unite.*

1. Why would it be challenging to balance on a *unicycle*?

   _____

2. What is a *unicorn* said to have on its forehead?

   _____

3. If two separate groups *unite*, what do they form?

   _____

© Pearson Education, Inc. All rights reserved.

"Popocatepetl and Ixtlaccihuatl" by Juliet Piggott Wood
Conventions: Punctuation Marks

Review ways that writers use the following common punctuation marks:

Punctuation/Usage	Example
colon (:) A *colon* introduces information that defines, explains, or provides a list of what is referred to before.	There are three main characters in the legend: the Emperor, his daughter, and the warrior she loves.
Semicolon (;) *Semicolons* can be used to join clauses in compound sentences.	One mountain is called Popocatepetl; the other one is called Ixtlaccihuatl.
Hyphen (-) A *hyphen* is used to join two or more separate words into a single word.	Both have snow-covered peaks, and the taller one is a still-active volcano.
Dash (—) *Dashes* are used to set off information that interrupts a thought.	Ixtlaccihuatl—or White Woman—is named after the Emperor's daughter.
Brackets ([ ]) *Brackets* are used to add clarifying information within a quotation.	"The Spaniards destroyed much of Tenochtitlan [the Aztec capital] and built another city in its place … Mexico City."
Parentheses (( )) *Parentheses* are used to include information in a sentence without changing the meaning of the sentence.	Many other warriors were jealous of Popo, the man whom Ixtla loved (Ixtla is short for Ixtlaccihuatl).

WRITING PRACTICE: *Each sentence is missing one or more punctuation marks. Rewrite each one with correct punctuation. There may be more than one way to punctuate some of the sentences.*

1. "He kept at bay kept away or outside those tribes living in and beyond the mountains surrounding the Valley of Mexico...."

_____

2. Finally, when the middle aged Emperor has almost given up, his wife gives birth to a daughter, their much loved only child.

_____

3. Ixtla is a smart, beautiful young woman all the young men in the city are in love with her.

_____

4. Ixtla loves one of her father's warriors Popo is his name but her father will not let her marry him.

_____

5. What happens at the end is tragic both Ixtla and Popo die like Romeo and Juliet in the Shakespeare play.

_____

All-in-One Workbook
© Pearson Education, Inc. All rights reserved.
244

"Popocatepetl and Ixtlaccihuatl" by Juliet Piggott Wood
Support for Writing to Sources: Description

Use this chart to take notes as you prepare to write a **description** of Ixtla. Write down as many details as you can to describe the various aspects of Ixtla's character. Include verbs and adjectives that appeal to the five senses: sight, touch, taste, smell, and hearing.

Background information about Ixtla (Who is she? What is she like? What is expected of her?):
Physical description of Ixtla:
Activities in which Ixtla takes part:

Now, use your notes to write a draft of a description of the character of Ixtla. Be sure to use vivid verbs and adjectives that will make your description interesting to your readers. Use words that appeal to the senses of sight, touch, taste, smell, and hearing.

© Pearson Education, Inc. All rights reserved.

"Popocatepetl and Ixtlaccihuatl" by Juliet Piggott Wood
Support for Speaking and Listening: Persuasive Speech

Respond to the following prompts as you prepare a **persuasive speech** aimed at convincing the Emperor that Popo and Ixtla should be allowed to marry.

Explanation of position: _____

_____

_____

Main points in support of position (solid evidence that will appeal to Emperor's emotions and sense of reason): _____

_____

_____

_____

_____

_____

_____

_____

_____

Phrases that will remind me of my points: _____

_____

_____

_____

_____

_____

_____

_____

Once you have organized your material, transfer your notes to cards that you can refer to as you deliver your speech.

© Pearson Education, Inc. All rights reserved.

"Sun and Moon in a Box" by Richard Erdoes and Alfonso Ortiz

Writing About the Big Question

Community or individual: Which is more important?

Big Question Vocabulary

common	community	culture	custom	diversity
duty	environment	ethnicity	family	group
individual	team	tradition	unify	unique

A. *Use one or more words from the list above to complete each sentence.*

1. Jesse and his friends joined a local fundraising _____.

2. The money raised would help protect the _____ and local wildlife.

3. The friends enjoyed working together toward a _____ goal.

4. They decided to make it an annual _____ .

B. *Follow the directions in responding to each of the items below.*

1. List two different times when you worked with others as part of a team.

   _____

   _____

2. Write two or three sentences describing one of the preceding experiences and explaining how it affected those involved. Use at least two of the Big Question vocabulary words. _____

   _____

   _____

   _____

C. *Complete the sentence below. Then, write a short paragraph in which you connect this idea to the big question.*

In order for people to work together as part of a team, they must _____

_____

_____

_____

_____

_____

_____

© Pearson Education, Inc. All rights reserved.

Name _____ Date _____

"Sun and Moon in a Box" by Richard Erdoes and Alfonso Ortiz

Reading: Use Prior Knowledge to Compare and Contrast

A **comparison** tells how two or more things are alike. A **contrast** tells how two or more things are different. When you **compare and contrast,** you recognize similarities and differences. You can often understand an unfamiliar concept by **using your prior knowledge to compare and contrast.** For example, you may understand an ancient culture better if you look for ways in which it is similar to and different from your own culture. You also might find similarities and differences between a story told long ago and one that is popular today. To compare and contrast stories, ask questions such as "What does this event bring to mind?" or "Does this character make me think of someone I know or have read about?"

DIRECTIONS: *Read each passage from "Sun and Moon in a Box." In the second column of the chart, write a question that will help you compare or contrast the passage to something else you have read or to something or someone you know or know about. In the third column, write the answer to your question. The first item has been completed as an example.*

Passage from "Sun and Moon in a Box"	Question Based on My Prior Knowledge	Comparison or Contrast
1. Coyote and Eagle were hunting. Eagle caught rabbits. Coyote caught nothing but grasshoppers. Coyote said, "Friend Eagle, my chief, we make a great hunting pair."	How are these characters like Wile E. Coyote and Road Runner in the cartoons I used to watch?	Road Runner is a bird, but not an eagle, and Wile E. Coyote tries to catch him. Here, the coyote and the eagle seem to be friends.
2. Whenever [the Kachinas] wanted light they opened the lid and let the sun peek out. Then, it was day. When they wanted less light, they opened the box just a little for the moon to look out.		
3. After a while Coyote called Eagle, "My chief, let me have the box. I am ashamed to let you do all the carrying." "No," said Eagle, "You are not reliable. You might be curious and open the box."		
4. [Coyote] sat down and opened the box. In a flash, . . . icy winds made all living things shiver. Then, before Coyote could put the lid back, . . . snow fell down from heaven and covered the plains and the mountains.		

"Sun and Moon in a Box" by Richard Erdoes and Alfonso Ortiz
Literary Analysis: Cultural Context

Stories such as fables, folk tales, and myths are influenced by cultural context. **Cultural context** is the background, customs, and beliefs of the people who originally told them. Knowing the cultural context of a work will help you understand and appreciate it. You can keep track of the cultural context of a work by considering these elements: the *title* of the selection, the *time* in which it takes place, the *place* in which it takes place, the *customs* of the characters, the *beliefs* that are expressed or suggested.

Consider this passage from "Sun and Moon in a Box":

Now, at this time, the earth was still soft and new. There was as yet no sun and no moon.

The passage tells you that the folk tale is set in the distant past, before Earth looked as it does today and before there was a sun and a moon. From the cultural context, you can infer that the people who told the tale believed there was a time when Earth existed, but the sun and the moon as yet did not.

DIRECTIONS: *Read each passage from "Sun and Moon in a Box." In the second column of the chart, indicate which element of the cultural context—time, place, customs, or beliefs—the passage illustrates. Then, explain your choice. Tell why you think the example shows the element you have chosen.*

Passage from "Sun and Moon in a Box"	Element of Cultural Context and Explanation
1. [Eagle and Coyote] went toward the west. They came to a deep canyon.	
2. Whenever [the Kachinas] wanted light they opened the lid and let the sun peek out. . . . When they wanted less light, they opened the box just a little for the moon to look out.	
3. "Let us steal the box," said Coyote. "No, that would be wrong," said Eagle. "Let us just borrow it."	
4. Eagle grabbed the box and . . . Coyote ran after him on the ground. After a while Coyote called Eagle: "My chief, let me have the box. I am ashamed to let you do all the carrying."	

Name _____ Date _____

"Sun and Moon in a Box" by Richard Erdoes and Alfonso Ortiz
Vocabulary Builder

Word List

cunning   pestering   regretted   relented   reliable

A. DIRECTIONS: *Circle* T *if the statement is* true *or* F *if it is* false. *Then, explain your answer.*

1. A car that starts only half the time is *reliable.*

   T / F _____

   _____

2. A teacher who refuses her students' pleas to make a test easier has *relented.*

   T / F _____

   _____

3. Someone who always gets caught cheating is *cunning.*

   T / F _____

   _____

4. A man who thoroughly disliked a movie, probably *regretted* going to see it.

   T / F _____

   _____

5. Parents would be charmed by a child who is *pestering* them.

   T / F _____

   _____

B. WORD STUDY: *The Latin suffix* -ity *means "state, quality, or condition of." Answer each of the following questions using one of these words containing* -ity: *elasticity, sincerity, predictability.*

1. How might you test an object's *elasticity*?

   _____

2. What might lead you to question a person's *sincerity*?

   _____

3. Why might you appreciate a coworker's *predictability*?

   _____

All-in-One Workbook
© Pearson Education, Inc. All rights reserved.
250

"Sun and Moon in a Box" by Alfonso Ortiz and Richard Erdoes
Conventions: Commas

A **comma** signals a brief pause. You should use a comma in these situations:

Use a Comma or Commas . . .	Example
before a conjunction that joins independent clauses in a compound sentence	Our library is full of books, but it also has many other materials.
after an introductory word, phrase, or clause	Wow, what a lot of shelves there are! At first, I couldn't even find my way around. Entering the library, you turn left for fiction.
to separate three or more words, phrases, or clauses in a series	The library offers magazines, movies on DVDs, and recorded books on CDs.
to separate **coordinate adjectives** (adjectives in a row that each separately modify the same noun). Writers often use the word *and* to link coordinate adjectives smoothly together.	Many creative, talented, and generous artists have donated paintings for display. These colorful, cheerful works brighten up the library's white walls.

A. DIRECTIONS: *Circle the letter of the sentence that uses commas correctly.*

1. A. The library offers separate sections for fiction, nonfiction, and reference.
   B. The library offers separate sections for fiction, nonfiction and reference.

2. A. In addition, there are separate sections for children and young adults.
   B. In addition there are separate sections for children, and young adults.

B. DIRECTIONS: *Rewrite this paragraph with commas inserted or removed wherever necessary.*

After the federal government cut money to the states most state county and local governments had budget problems. Many library services, and other local services had to be cut back. Hoping to help a group of people began Bookworms an organization that is raising funds for the local library. One of the first things Bookworms organized, was a book magazine, and DVD sale. Local residents donated used materials and the money from the sale went to the library.

_____

_____

_____

_____

_____

_____

Name _____ Date _____

Use this chart to take notes for a **plot summary** of "Sun and Moon in a Box."

Setting:		
Major character 1: _____ _____ _____ _____		**Major character 2:** _____ _____ _____ _____
Main event from beginning of folk tale: _____ _____ _____ _____ _____ _____ _____ _____ _____ _____ _____ _____ _____	**Main event from middle of folk tale:** _____ _____ _____ _____ _____ _____ _____ _____ _____ _____ _____ _____ _____	**Main event from end of folk tale:** _____ _____ _____ _____ _____ _____ _____ _____ _____ _____ _____ _____ _____
Final outcome:		

You can use your notes to write your **plot summary.** Be sure to include all the information called for in the chart.

"Sun and Moon in a Box" by Richard Erdoes and Alfonso Ortiz
Support for Speaking and Listening: Story

Use the following prompts as you work with a partner to gather unusual facts about an animal in preparation for a **story** you will make up and present to your classmates. Remember: You will not name the animal in your presentation.

Unusual fact 1: _____

_____

Unusual fact 2: _____

_____

Unusual fact 3: _____

_____

Unusual fact 4: _____

_____

Unusual fact 5: _____

_____

Facial expressions, gestures, and movements that identify the animal: _____

_____

_____

_____

_____

_____

_____

_____

Dialogue: _____

_____

_____

_____

_____

_____

_____

_____

_____

© Pearson Education, Inc. All rights reserved.

"The People Could Fly" by Virginia Hamilton
Writing About the Big Question

Community or individual: Which is more important?

Big Question Vocabulary

common	community	culture	custom	diversity
duty	environment	ethnicity	family	group
individual	team	tradition	unify	unique

A. *Use one or more words from the list above to complete each sentence.*

1. America has not always embraced the _____ of its population.

2. Some people were discriminated against because of their _____.

3. When people came together as a _____ , they made a difference.

4. There was power in their _____ that could not be denied.

B. *Follow the directions in responding to each of the items below.*

1. List two different groups of people who struggled against oppression.

   _____   _____

2. Write two sentences describing what helped unify one of the preceding groups in their efforts. Use at least two of the Big Question vocabulary words.

   _____

   _____

   _____

C. *Complete the sentence below. Then, write a short paragraph in which you connect this situation to the big question.*

In order to unify people who share a common struggle, _____

_____

_____

_____

_____

_____

_____

_____

All-in-One Workbook
© Pearson Education, Inc. All rights reserved.
254

Name _____ Date _____

"The People Could Fly" by Virginia Hamilton

Reading: Use a Venn Diagram to Compare and Contrast

When you **compare and contrast,** you recognize similarities and differences. You can compare and contrast elements in a literary work by **using a Venn diagram** to examine character traits, situations, and ideas. First, reread the text to locate the details you will compare. Then, write the details on a diagram like the ones shown below. Recording these details will help you understand the similarities and differences in a literary work.

DIRECTIONS: *Fill in the Venn diagrams as directed to make comparisons about elements of "The People Could Fly."*

1. Compare Toby and Sarah. Write characteristics of Toby in the left-hand oval and characteristics of Sarah in the right-hand oval. Write characteristics that they share in the overlapping part of the two ovals.

Toby   **Both**   **Sarah**

2. Compare the enslaved people with the Overseer and Driver. Write characteristics of the enslaved people in the left-hand oval and characteristics of the Overseer and Driver in the right-hand oval. Write characteristics that they share in the overlapping part of the two ovals.

Enslaved People   **Both**   **Overseer and Driver**

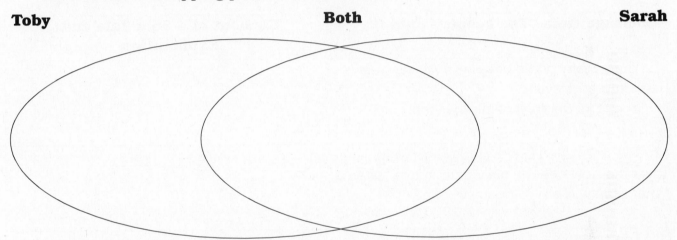

"**The People Could Fly**" by Virginia Hamilton
Literary Analysis: Folk Tale

A **folk tale** is a story that is composed orally and then passed from person to person by word of mouth. Although folk tales originate in this **oral tradition,** many of them are eventually collected and written down. Similar folk tales are told by different cultures throughout the world. Such folk tales have common character types, plot elements, and themes. Folk tales often teach a lesson about life and present a clear separation between good and evil. Folk tales are part of the oral tradition that also includes fairy tales, legends, myths, fables, tall tales, and ghost stories.

DIRECTIONS: *Read each passage from "The People Could Fly." In the second column of the chart, indicate whether the passage* teaches a lesson about life *or whether it* clearly presents good, clearly presents evil, *or presents a clear distinction between the two. Then, explain your choice. Tell why you think the example shows the element you have chosen.*

Passage from "The People Could Fly"	Element of a Folk Tale and Explanation
1. Then, many of the people [in Africa] were captured for Slavery. . . . The folks were full of misery, then.	
2. The one called Driver cracked his whip over the slow ones to make them move faster. That whip was a slice-open cut of pain.	
3. The . . . woman fell to the earth. The old man that was there, Toby, came and helped her to her feet.	
4. A young man slave fell from the heat. The Driver come and whipped him. Toby come over and spoke words to the fallen one.	
5. "Take us with you!" . . . Toby couldn't take them with him. Hadn't the time to teach them to fly. They must wait for a chance to run.	
6. The slaves who could not fly told about the people who could fly to their children. When they were free.	

© Pearson Education, Inc. All rights reserved.

Name _____ Date _____

"The People Could Fly" by Virginia Hamilton
Vocabulary Builder

Word List

croon   hoed   scorned   shed   shuffle

A. DIRECTIONS: *Write the letter of the word or group of words that means the opposite of the vocabulary word.*

____ 1. scorned
   A. commanded   **B.** resigned   **C.** appreciated   **D.** hired

____ 2. croon
   A. sing softly   **B.** speak quietly   **C.** speak haltingly **D.** sing loudly

____ 3. shuffle
   A. jump   **B.** walk quickly   **C.** drag   **D.** pull into

____ 4. shed
   A. put on   **B.** pull down   **C.** take off   **D.** drop

____ 5. hoed
   A. dug   **B.** straightened   **C.** released   **D.** planted

B. WORD STUDY: *The Greek root -myst- means "a secret rite." Answer each of the following questions using one of these words containing -myst-: mystified, mystical, mystic.*

1. How would you reply if you were *mystified* by a friend's request?

   _____

   _____

2. When might an ancient artifact be considered a *mystical* object?

   _____

   _____

3. Why might someone seek guidance from a *mystic*?

   _____

   _____

"The People Could Fly" by Virginia Hamilton
Conventions: Capitalization

Capitalization is the use of uppercase letters (*A*, *B*, *C*, and so on). Capital letters signal the beginning of a sentence or a quotation and identify proper nouns and proper adjectives. **Proper nouns** include the names of people, geographical locations, specific events and time periods, organizations, languages, and religions. **Proper adjectives** are derived from proper nouns.

Use of Capital Letters	Example
Beginnings of sentences	The people could fly. They looked like blackbirds.
Quotations	The Overseer called, "Keep that thing quiet."
Proper nouns	They forgot how to fly as they sailed away from Africa.
Proper adjectives	The tale's setting is a plantation in the South.

A. PRACTICE: *Rewrite each sentence below. Use capitalization correctly.*

1. the character named toby still knows how to fly.

   _____

2. the folk tale takes place in the american south before the civil war, perhaps in georgia or mississippi.

   _____

   _____

3. "i must go soon," sarah tells toby.

   _____

4. but toby just laughs. he throws back his head and says, "hee, hee! don't you know who i am?"

   _____

B. Writing Application: *Write a short episode telling what the Master's and the Overseer's reactions might be after the people fly away. Include at least one quotation, one proper noun, and one proper adjective. Use capitalization correctly.*

_____

_____

_____

_____

_____

"The People Could Fly" by Virginia Hamilton
Support for Writing to Sources: Review

Use this chart to take notes for a **review** of "The People Could Fly."

Notes for Review

Element of the Tale	My Opinion of the Element	Details From the Tale That Support My Opinion
Characters		
Description		
Dialogue		
Plot		

Now, write a draft of your review. Tell readers whether or not you think they will enjoy the folk tale. Remember to support your opinions with details from the tale.

© Pearson Education, Inc. All rights reserved.

Name _____ Date _____

Support for Speaking and Listening: Television News Report

Use the following prompts to prepare a **television news report** on the amazing events that took place in " The People Could Fly." Respond to the prompts with details from the folktale.

Where events took place: _____

_____

When events took place: _____

What happened: _____

_____

_____

_____

_____

_____

Question for Eyewitness: _____

_____

_____

_____

Eyewitness's answer: _____

_____

_____

_____

Question for Eyewitness: _____

_____

_____

Eyewitness's answer: _____

_____

_____

_____

"To the Top of Everest" by Samantha Larson
"The Voyage from Tales from the Odyssey" by Mary Pope Osborne
Writing About the Big Question

Community or individual: Which is more important?

Big Question Vocabulary

common	community	culture	custom	diversity
duty	environment	ethnicity	family	group
individual	team	tradition	unify	unique

A. *Use one or more words from the list above to complete each sentence.*

1. The _____ of rock climbers prepared for their journey.

2. They had a _____ goal of reaching the summit.

3. They were awed by the _____ of flora and fauna around them.

4. They felt fortunate to be in such a beautiful _____ .

B. *Follow the directions in responding to each of the items below.*

1. List two times when you traveled to a new place. _____ .
_____

2. Write two sentences describing one of the preceding experiences, and explain how it affected your view of the world. Use at least two of the Big Question vocabulary words.
_____
_____

C. *Complete the sentence below. Then, write a short paragraph in which you connect this idea to the big question.*

Travel enriches an individual's view of the world. A community of travelers

_____
_____
_____
_____
_____
_____

© Pearson Education, Inc. All rights reserved.

"To the Top of Everest" by Samantha Larson
"The Voyage from Tales from the Odyssey" by Mary Pope Osborne
Literary Analysis: Comparing Universal Themes

A universal theme is a message about life that is expressed regularly in many different cultures and time periods. Universal themes include the importance of courage, the power of love, and the danger of greed. Universal themes are often found in epics, or stories or long poems about the adventures of a larger-than-life hero. Epic tales usually focus on the hero's bravery, strength, and success in battle or adventure. In addition to telling the story of a hero, an epic is a portrait of the culture that produced it. The following **epic conventions** are traditional characteristics of this form of literature:

- An epic involves a dangerous journey, or *quest*, that the hero must take.
- Gods or powerful characters help the hero.
- The setting of an epic is broad, covering several nations or even the universe.
- The style is serious and formal.

Because epics have become an important part of the literature of different cultures, they often inspire the works of later generations. For example, it is not unusual to find an allusion, or reference, to the ancient Greek epic the *Odyssey* in a contemporary adventure story. As you read "To the Top of Everest" and "The Voyage from Tales from the Odyssey," look for the use of epic conventions in the stories.

DIRECTIONS: *Use the following chart to compare "To the Top of Everest" and "The Voyage from Tales from the Odyssey." If the information to answer a question does not appear in the selection, write* information not mentioned.

Questions	"To the Top of Everest"	"The Voyage from Tales from the Odyssey"
1. What is the setting?		
2. What dangerous journey is undertaken?		
3. Who helps along the journey?		
4. What is the character's attitude?		
5. What obstacles must be overcome?		
6. What is the outcome?		

Name _____ Date _____

"To the Top of Everest" by Samantha Larson
"The Voyage from Tales from the Odyssey" by Mary Pope Osborne
Vocabulary Builder

Word List

designated   impervious   inflicted   saturation

A. DIRECTIONS: *Think about the meaning of each italicized word from the Word List. Then, explain whether the sentence makes sense. If it does not make sense, write a new sentence. In the new sentence, use the italicized word correctly.*

1. Jenna *inflicted* comfort with her gentle touch.

   Explanation: _____

   New sentence: _____

2. The leaky bottle resulted in the *saturation* of Emma's cotton bib.

   Explanation: _____

   New sentence: _____

3. We *designated* our star player as our choice for team captain.

   Explanation: _____

   New sentence: _____

4. Her proud smile suggested she was *impervious* to our compliments.

   Explanation: _____

   New sentence: _____

B. DIRECTIONS: *Write the letter of the word that means* the same or about the same *as the word from the Word List.*

____ 1. designated
    A. designed   C. described
    B. arranged   D. marked

____ 2. impervious
    A. unaffected   C. lazy
    B. angry   D. bored

____ 3. inflicted
    A. stopped   C. caused
    B. soothed   D. increased

Name _____ Date _____

Support for Writing to Compare Universal Themes

Use this graphic organizer to take notes for an essay in which you compare and contrast the themes of "To the Top of Everest" and "The Voyage from Tales from the Odyssey."

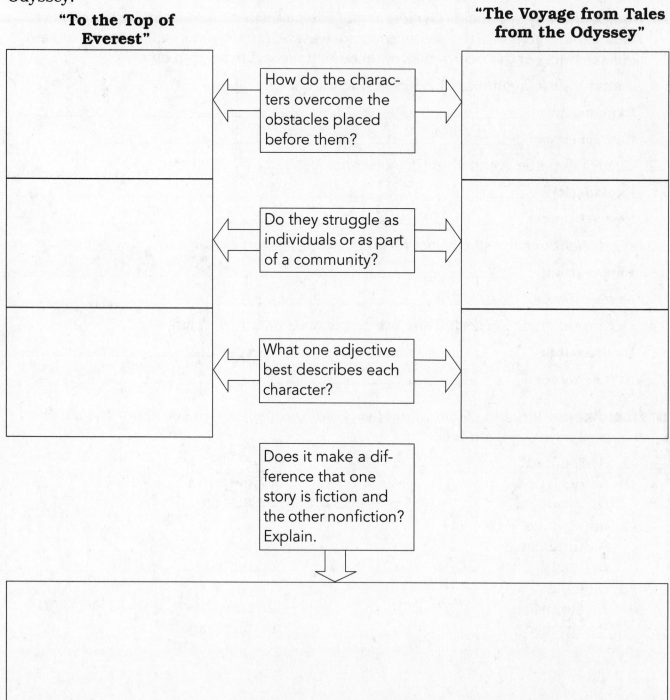

"To the Top of Everest"

"The Voyage from Tales from the Odyssey"

How do the characters overcome the obstacles placed before them?

Do they struggle as individuals or as part of a community?

What one adjective best describes each character?

Does it make a difference that one story is fiction and the other nonfiction? Explain.

Now, use your notes to write an essay comparing and contrasting the themes of "To the Top of Everest" and "The Voyage from Tales from the Odyssey."

All-in-One Workbook
© Pearson Education, Inc. All rights reserved.

Name _____ Date _____

Cause-and-Effect Essay

Prewriting: Narrowing Your Topic

Use the following web to narrow your topic. Write your topic in the center, surround it with subtopics, and list causes and effects connected to each subtopic.

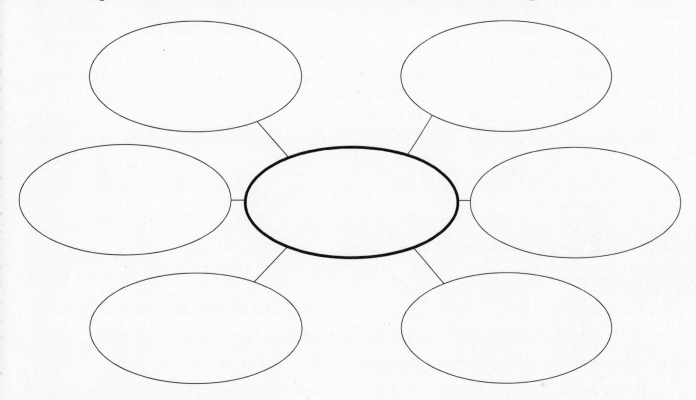

Drafting: Organizing Your Essay

List the main points of your cause-and-effect essay in the following graphic organizer.

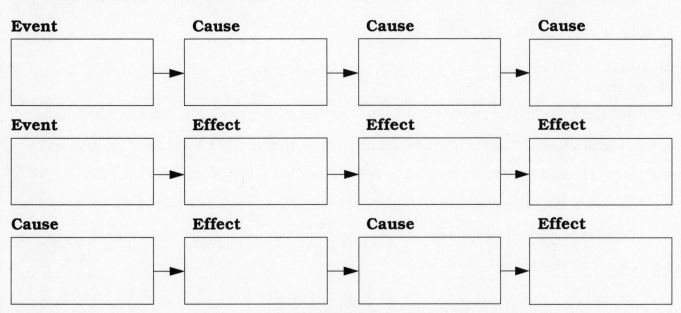

© Pearson Education, Inc. All rights reserved.

Writer's Toolbox
Conventions: Revising Incorrect Use of Commas

A **comma** signals a brief pause. You should use a comma in these situations:

before a conjunction that separates two independent clauses in a compound sentence	Our library is full of books, but it also has many other materials.
between items in a series	The library offers magazines, CDs, and DVDs.
between adjectives of equal rank that modify the same noun or pronoun (If the word *and* can replace the comma, the adjectives are of equal rank)	The old library was a large, ugly building.
to set off introductory words, phrases, or clauses	Entering the library, you turn left for fiction.
to set off words, phrases, and clauses that interrupt a sentence	Mrs. Lee, the librarian, is very helpful.

Identifying Correct Use of Commas

A. DIRECTIONS: *Circle the letter of the sentence that uses commas correctly.*

1. A. The library offers separate sections for fiction, nonfiction, and reference.

   B. The library offers separate sections for fiction, nonfiction and reference.

2. A. In addition, there are separate sections for children and young adults.

   B. In addition there are separate sections for children, and young adults.

3. A. When Mr. Van my neighbor, visits the library he researches his family tree.

   B. When Mr. Van, my neighbor, visits the library, he researches his family tree.

Fixing Incorrect Use of Commas

B. DIRECTIONS: *Rewrite this paragraph with commas inserted or removed wherever necessary.*

After the federal government cut money to the states most state county and local governments had budget problems. Many libraries, and other local services had to be cut back. Hoping to help a group of people began Bookworms an organization that is raising funds for the local library. One of the first things Bookworms organized, was an art show. Many creative, talented, artists donated their works and the money from the sales went to the library.

Name _____ Date _____

"My First Free Summer" by Julia Alvarez
Vocabulary Builder

Selection Vocabulary

    contradiction   summoned   vowed

A. DIRECTIONS: *Write at least one synonym, one antonym, and an example sentence for each word. Synonyms and antonyms can be words or phrases.*

Word	Synonym	Antonym	Example Sentence
vowed			
summoned			
contradiction			

Academic Vocabulary

    culture   explain   perspective

B. DIRECTIONS: *Complete each sentence with a word, phrase, or clause that contains a context clue for the italicized word.*

1. The instructor tried to *explain* how to use the equipment, but Sean _____

    _____.

2. Yvonne told the story from her own *perspective* so _____

    _____.

3. Every *culture* has strong traditions that _____

    _____.

© Pearson Education, Inc. All rights reserved.

Name _____ Date _____

"My First Free Summer" by Julia Alvarez
Take Notes for Discussion

Before the Group Discussion: Read the following passage from the selection.

> The summer of 1960 began in bliss: I did not have to go to summer
> school! *Attitude much improved. Her English progressing nicely. Attentive*
> *and cooperative in classroom.* I grinned as Mami read off the note that
> accompanied my report card of Bs.

During the Discussion: As you discuss each question, take notes on how other
students' ideas either differ from or build upon your own.

Discussion Questions	Other Ideas Expressed	Comparison to My Own Ideas
1. How does Alvarez finally escape summer school?		
2. Is it usually beneficial for a person to do what is expected of him or her? When may it not be beneficial?		

© Pearson Education, Inc. All rights reserved.

"My First Free Summer" by Julia Alvarez
Take Notes for Writing to Sources

Planning Your Informative Text: Before you begin drafting your **comparison-and-contrast essay,** use the chart below to organize your ideas. Follow the directions at the top of each section.

1. Identify the main focus of your essay, and then state your main idea. You will use this statement in your introduction.

_____

_____

_____

_____

_____

2. List specific examples from the text that support your main idea and show how Alvarez felt *before* she left for the United States.

_____

_____

_____

_____

_____

_____

_____

_____

3. List specific examples from the text that support your main idea and show how Alvarez felt *after* she left for the United States.

_____

_____

_____

_____

_____

_____

_____

_____

© Pearson Education, Inc. All rights reserved.

Name _____ Date _____

"My First Free Summer" by Julia Alvarez
Take Notes for Research

As you research **the different reasons people immigrate to the United States,** use the forms below to take notes from your sources. As necessary, continue your notes on the back of this page, on note cards, or in a word-processing document.

Source Information   Check one: ☐ Primary Source   ☐ Secondary Source

Title: _____   Author: _____

Publication Information: _____

Page(s): _____

Main Idea: _____

_____

Quotation or Paraphrase: _____

_____

Source Information   Check one: ☐ Primary Source   ☐ Secondary Source

Title: _____   Author: _____

Publication Information: _____

Page(s): _____

Main Idea: _____

_____

Quotation or Paraphrase: _____

_____

Source Information   Check one: ☐ Primary Source   ☐ Secondary Source

Title: _____   Author: _____

Publication Information: _____

Page(s): _____

Main Idea: _____

_____

Quotation or Paraphrase: _____

_____

© Pearson Education, Inc. All rights reserved.

Name _____ Date _____

"How I Learned English" by Gregory Djanikian
Vocabulary Builder

Selection Vocabulary

notions   transfixed   writhing

A. DIRECTIONS: *Decide whether each statement below is true or false. On the line before each item, write TRUE or FALSE. Then explain your answers.*

_____ 1. It was my *notion* to turn off the game and go find somebody to play basketball with.

_____.

_____ 2. Eager to finish her shopping, Sarah ran *transfixed* into the last store to make her purchase.

_____.

_____ 3. *Writhing* with boredom, he tried to keep his eyes open and finish reading.

_____.

Academic Vocabulary

explain   outcome   stanza

B. DIRECTIONS: *Write a complete sentence to answer each question. For each item, use a vocabulary word from the list in place of the underlined words with similar meanings.*

1. What was one <u>result</u> of the speaker's game of baseball in "How I Learned English"?

_____

_____

2. A <u>verse</u> in poetry resembles what in a prose essay?

_____

_____

3. Who do most students ask to <u>clarify</u> points of grammar and usage.

_____

_____

All-in-One Workbook
© Pearson Education, Inc. All rights reserved.
271

Name _____ Date _____

"How I Learned English" by Gregory Djanikian
Take Notes for Discussion

Before the Partner Discussion: Read the following passage from the selection.

Someone said "shin" again…And dusting me off with hands like swatters.

During the Discussion: As you discuss each question, take notes on how your partner's ideas either differ from or build upon your own.

Discussion Questions	Other Ideas Expressed	Comparison to My Own Ideas
1. Why does the speaker think it is important that he joined in the laughter?		
2. How might the **outcome** of the day have been different if the speaker had not been hit in the head or if he had been angered by the boys' laughter?		

© Pearson Education, Inc. All rights reserved.

Name _____ Date _____

"**How I Learned English**" by Gregory Djanikian
Take Notes for Research

As you research **resources that help recent immigrants to the United States learn about their new home,** use the chart below to take notes from your sources. As necessary, continue your notes on the back of this page, on note cards, or in a word-processing document.

Resources for New Immigrants	
Main Idea _____ _____ Quotation or Paraphrase _____ _____ _____ _____ _____ Source Information _____ _____ _____ _____	Main Idea _____ _____ Quotation or Paraphrase _____ _____ _____ _____ _____ Source Information _____ _____ _____ _____
Main Idea _____ _____ Quotation or Paraphrase _____ _____ _____ _____ _____ Source Information _____ _____ _____ _____	Main Idea _____ _____ Quotation or Paraphrase _____ _____ _____ _____ _____ Source Information _____ _____ _____ _____

© Pearson Education, Inc. All rights reserved.

"How I Learned English" by Gregory Djanikian
Take Notes for Writing to Sources

Planning Your Autobiographical Narrative: Before you begin drafting your **autobiographical narrative,** use the chart below to organize your ideas. Follow the directions in each section.

1. List details about the time, place, and situation.

_____

_____

_____

_____

_____

2. Write notes about how you felt when you didn't fit in. Describe the outcome of the situation.

_____

_____

_____

_____

_____

_____

3. Jot ideas for including dialogue, characterization, and other story elements to bring the narrative alive.

_____

_____

_____

_____

_____

4. Write notes to use in your conclusion about what you learned.

_____

_____

_____

_____

_____

_____

© Pearson Education, Inc. All rights reserved.

"**mk**" by Jean Fritz
Vocabulary Builder

Selection Vocabulary

adequate   deceive   ignorant

A. DIRECTIONS: *Write the letter of the word or phrase that is the best antonym for the italicized word. Then use the italicized word in a complete sentence.*

_____ 1. *adequate*

   A. absent   C. enough

   B. insufficient   D. compassionate

_____

_____ 2. *deceive*

   A. mislead   C. educate

   B. yell   D. be loyal

_____

_____ 3. *ignorant*

   A. knowledgeable   C. curious

   B. uninformed   D. confident

_____

Academic Vocabulary

communicate   predict

B. DIRECTIONS: *Complete each sentence with a word, phrase, or clause that contains a context clue for the italicized word.*

1. Because I could not *communicate* with her, she _____

   _____.

2. The weather forecaster said a severe snowstorm is headed our way, and I *predict*
   that _____

   _____.

"mk" by Jean Fritz
Take Notes for Discussion

Before the Group Discussion: Read the following passage from the selection.

> I had the feeling that I was coming to the end of my quest. But not quite. One day when someone asked me where I was born, I found myself smiling. I was for the moment standing beside the Yangtze River. "My hometown," I said, "was Wuhan, China." I discovered that I had to take China with me wherever I went.

During the Discussion: As you discuss each question, take notes on how your partner's ideas either differ from or build upon your own.

Discussion Questions	Other Ideas Expressed	Comparison to My Own Ideas
1. Why did Fritz previously avoid mentioning the name of her hometown in China?		
2. Why was she finally able to name her hometown?		

© Pearson Education, Inc. All rights reserved.

Name _____ Date _____

"mk" by Jean Fritz
Take Notes for Research

As you research **why "The Courtship of Miles Standish" is important to American literature,** use the forms below to take notes from your sources. As necessary, continue your notes on the back of this page, on note cards, or in a word-processing document.

Source Information   Check one: ☐ Primary Source   ☐ Secondary Source

Title: _____   Author: _____

Publication Information: _____

Page(s): _____

Main Idea: _____

_____

Quotation or Paraphrase: _____

_____

Source Information   Check one: ☐ Primary Source   ☐ Secondary Source

Title: _____   Author: _____

Publication Information: _____

Page(s): _____

Main Idea: _____

_____

Quotation or Paraphrase: _____

_____

Source Information   Check one: ☐ Primary Source   ☐ Secondary Source

Title: _____   Author: _____

Publication Information: _____

Page(s): _____

Main Idea: _____

_____

Quotation or Paraphrase: _____

_____

"mk" by Jean Fritz

Take Notes for Writing to Sources

Planning Your Comparison-and-Contrast Essay: Before you begin drafting your **comparison-and-contrast essay,** use the chart below to organize your ideas. Follow the directions in each section.

1. State your main idea. You will use this statement in your introduction.

_____

_____

_____

2. Gather story details about Fritz's thoughts and feelings about America when she lived in China.

_____

_____

_____

_____

_____

_____

3. Gather story details about her thoughts and feelings when she lived in the U.S. List them in the order you'll discuss them.

_____

_____

_____

_____

_____

4. Jot down notes for your conclusion that will sum up your main idea and most important details.

_____

_____

_____

_____

Name _____ Date _____

"Discovering a Paper Son" by Byron Yee
Vocabulary Builder

Selection Vocabulary

decipher   interrogations   scrutiny

A. DIRECTIONS: *Write an explanation for your answer to each question. Be sure to use the italicized word in your sentence.*

1. What is an example of something that someone would want to *decipher*?

   _____.

2. Why might *interrogations* make some people anxious?

   _____.

3. Why would someone want to avoid close *scrutiny*?

   _____.

Academic Vocabulary

cites   discover   enhance

B. DIRECTIONS: *Complete each sentence with a word, phrase, or clause that contains a context clue for the italicized word.*

1. Olivia wanted to *discover* where her family came from so _____

   _____.

2. You might *enhance* a multimedia presentation by _____

   _____.

3. Cesar *cites* many sources for his information because _____

   _____.

Name _____ Date _____

"**Discovering a Paper Son**" by Byron Yee
Take Notes for Discussion

Before the Partner Discussion: Read the following passage from the selection.

"You see my story is no different from anyone else's…In all of our collective past, we've all had that one ancestor that had the strength to break from what was familiar to venture into the unknown."

During the Discussion: As you discuss each question, take notes on how your partner's ideas either differ from or build upon your own.

Discussion Questions	Other Ideas Expressed	Comparison to My Own Ideas
1. How did Bing Quai Yee display courage in his quest to become an American citizen?		
2. How is Byron Yee's story "no different from anyone else's"?		

© Pearson Education, Inc. All rights reserved.

Name _____   Date _____

"**Discovering a Paper Son**" by Byron Yee
Take Notes for Research

As you research **why the Chinese Exclusion Act was passed and when and why it was repealed,** you can use the organizer below to take notes from your sources. As necessary, continue your notes on the back of this page, on note cards, or in a word-processing document.

The Chinese Exclusion Act

Main Idea _____

_____

Quotation or Paraphrase _____

_____

_____

_____

Source Information _____

_____

_____

_____

Main Idea _____

_____

Quotation or Paraphrase _____

_____

_____

_____

Source Information _____

_____

_____

_____

Main Idea _____

_____

Quotation or Paraphrase _____

_____

_____

_____

Source Information _____

_____

_____

_____

Main Idea _____

_____

Quotation or Paraphrase _____

_____

_____

_____

Source Information _____

_____

_____

_____

Name _____ Date _____

"**Discovering a Paper Son**" by Byron Yee
Take Notes for Writing to Sources

Planning Your Informational Text: Before you begin drafting your **expository essay,** use the chart below to organize your ideas. Follow the directions in each section.

---

1. Write a thesis statement that you will include in your introduction.

_____

_____

_____

_____

---

2. List the chain of events that led up to Yee's admittance into the United States.

_____

_____

_____

_____

_____

_____

_____

_____

_____

_____

_____

_____

_____

_____

_____

---

3. Write notes for your conclusion that includes a summary of events and the causes for Yee's actions.

_____

_____

_____

_____

_____

_____

_____

Name _____ Date _____

from **Grandpa and the Statue** by Arthur Miller
Vocabulary Builder

Selection Vocabulary

peeved   subscribed   swindle

A. DIRECTIONS: *Provide an explanation for your answer to each question.*

1. If you *subscribed* to a magazine, why would you have to pay money for it?

_____

_____.

2. When someone is *peeved,* is he or she likely to speak bluntly? _____

_____.

3. If someone tries to *swindle* someone else, can that person be arrested? _____

_____.

Academic Vocabulary

characterize   debate   discover

B. DIRECTIONS: *Write the letter of the word or phrase that means the same or about the same as the vocabulary word. Then use the italicized word in a complete sentence.*

_____ 1. *characterize*

    A. imitate   **C.** imagine

    B. deny   **D.** describe

_____

_____ 2. *debate*

    A. argue   **C.** explain

    B. question   **D.** tell

_____

_____ 3. *discover*

    A. examine   **C.** find

    B. lose   **D.** investigate

_____

Name _____ Date _____

from **Grandpa and the Statue** by Arthur Miller
Take Notes for Discussion

Before the Debate: Read the following passage from the selection.

> MONAGHAN. That tablet there in her hand. What's it say? July Eye Vee [IV] MDCCLXXVI...what...what's all that?

> SHEEAN. That means July 4, 1776. It's in Roman numbers. Very high class.

> MONAGHAN. What's the good of it? If they're going to put a sign on her they ought to put it: Welcome All. That's it. Welcome All.

During the Debate: As you discuss and debate each question, take notes on how other students' ideas either differ from or build upon your own.

Discussion Questions	Other Ideas Expressed	Comparison to My Own Ideas
1. Why does Monaghan object to the Roman numbers on the tablet the statue holds?	_____ _____ _____ _____ _____ _____	_____ _____ _____ _____ _____ _____
2. What does Sheean think of the tablet?	_____ _____ _____ _____ _____ _____	_____ _____ _____ _____ _____ _____
3. What different attitudes about coming to the United States do these opinions show?	_____ _____ _____ _____ _____ _____	_____ _____ _____ _____ _____ _____

from **Grandpa and the Statue** by Arthur Miller
Take Notes for Research

As you research **Emma Lazarus and her poem,** use the forms below to take notes from your sources. As necessary, continue your notes on the back of this page, on note cards, or in a word-processing document.

Source Information   Check one: ☐ Primary Source   ☐ Secondary Source

Title: _____   Author: _____

Publication Information: _____

Page(s): _____

Main Idea: _____

_____

Quotation or Paraphrase: _____

_____

Source Information   Check one: ☐ Primary Source   ☐ Secondary Source

Title: _____   Author: _____

Publication Information: _____

Page(s): _____

Main Idea: _____

_____

Quotation or Paraphrase: _____

_____

Source Information   Check one: ☐ Primary Source   ☐ Secondary Source

Title: _____   Author: _____

Publication Information: _____

Page(s): _____

Main Idea: _____

_____

Quotation or Paraphrase: _____

_____

© Pearson Education, Inc. All rights reserved.

from **Grandpa and the Statue** by Arthur Miller
Take Notes for Writing to Sources

Planning Your Explanatory Essay: Before you begin drafting your **explanatory essay,** use the chart below to organize your ideas. Follow the directions at the top of each section of the chart.

1. Write a thesis statement stating your claim about which character makes the better claim. You will use this statement in your introduction.

_____

_____

_____

_____

2. List evidence from the play that supports your thesis statement.

_____

_____

_____

_____

_____

_____

_____

_____

_____

_____

_____

_____

3. Write notes you can use in your conclusion. Consider how you can make it memorable and satisfying.

_____

_____

_____

_____

Name _____ Date _____

"Melting Pot" by Anna Quindlen
Vocabulary Builder

Selection Vocabulary

bigots   dolefully   fluent

A. DIRECTIONS: *Write at least one synonym, one antonym, and an example sentence for each word. Synonyms and antonyms can be words or phrases.*

Word	Synonym	Antonym	Example Sentence
fluent			
bigots			
dolefully			

Academic Vocabulary

attitude   community   compose

B. DIRECTIONS: *Read each sentence. If the italicized word is used correctly, write* Correct *on the line. If it is not used correctly, rewrite the sentence to correct it.*

1. Recent immigrants may find it difficult to fit into their new *community*. _____

_____.

2. The unpleasant *attitude* of their neighbors made them eager to meet everyone.

_____

_____.

3. Madison couldn't *compose* the poem, so she turned it in as it was. _____

_____.

Name _____   Date _____

"Melting Pot" by Anna Quindlen
Take Notes for Discussion

Before the Discussion: Read the following passage from the selection.

Drawn in broad strokes, we live in a pressure cooker: oil and water, us and
them. But if you come around at exactly the right time, you'll find members
of all these groups gathered around complaining about the condition of the
streets, on which everyone can agree. We melt together, then draw apart.
I am the granddaughter of immigrants, a young professional—either an
interloper or a longtime resident, depending on your concept of time. I am
one of them, and one of us.

During the Discussion: As you discuss each question, take notes on how other
students' ideas either differ from or build upon your own.

Discussion Questions	Other Ideas Expressed	Comparison to My Own Ideas
1. According to Quindlen, what can bring different groups of people together?		
2. Why might a person feel as if he or she is part of more than just one group of people?		

© Pearson Education, Inc. All rights reserved.

Name _____ Date _____

Take Notes for Research

As you research **U.S. cities with large immigrant populations,** use the organizer below to take notes from your sources. As necessary, continue your notes on the back of this page, on note cards, or in a word-processing document.

Cities with Large Immigrant Populations	
Main Idea _____ _____ **Quotation or Paraphrase** _____ _____ _____ _____ _____ **Source Information** _____ _____ _____ _____ _____	**Main Idea** _____ _____ **Quotation or Paraphrase** _____ _____ _____ _____ _____ **Source Information** _____ _____ _____ _____ _____
Main Idea _____ _____ **Quotation or Paraphrase** _____ _____ _____ _____ _____ **Source Information** _____ _____ _____ _____ _____	**Main Idea** _____ _____ **Quotation or Paraphrase** _____ _____ _____ _____ _____ **Source Information** _____ _____ _____ _____ _____

© Pearson Education, Inc. All rights reserved.

"Melting Pot" by Anna Quindlen
Take Notes for Writing to Sources

Planning Your Argumentative Text: Before you begin drafting your **problem-and-solution essay,** use the chart below to organize your ideas. Follow the directions in each section.

---

1. State your thesis in which you propose solutions and explain why they will work.

_____

_____

_____

---

2. List your reasons, facts, and other evidence from the text and from your own experience to support your thesis.

_____

_____

_____

_____

_____

_____

_____

_____

_____

_____

_____

---

3. Jot notes for your conclusion. Summarize your solution and restate the main reasons it will work.

_____

_____

_____

_____

_____

_____

_____

Name _____ Date _____

Academic Vocabulary

individual

DIRECTIONS: *Complete this word map by writing a synonym, an antonym, and an example sentence in the appropriate boxes.*

Academic Vocabulary

Word Map

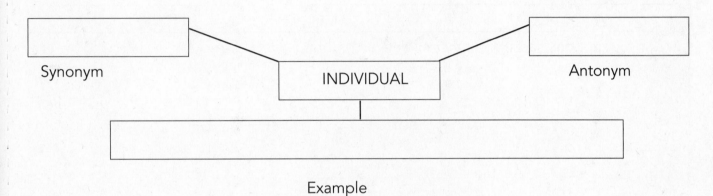

	INDIVIDUAL	
Synonym		Antonym

Example

Take Notes for Research

As you research the **current immigration process for people who want to move to the U.S.,** use the forms below to take notes from your sources. As necessary, continue your notes on the back of this page, on note cards, or in a word-processing document.

Source Information Check one: ☐ Primary Source ☐ Secondary Source

Title: _____ Author: _____

Publication Information: _____

Page(s): _____

Main Idea: _____

_____

Quotation or Paraphrase: _____

_____

© Pearson Education, Inc. All rights reserved.